THE INVISIBLE WAR

Cybersecurity in the Age of Exposure

How to Protect Your Identity, Your Business, Your Reputation, and Your Trust in a World That Never Stops Watching

By M.L.

A Book in The Invisible War Series

The Invisible War: Cybersecurity in the Age of Exposure

This book is published by

:

Trient Press®

1295 Grands Summit Dr, Suite B112

Reno, NV 89523

United States

Trient Press® is a registered trademark and legally owned company operating under the laws of the State of Nevada. All rights in the Trient Press® name, mark, and associated publishing identity are reserved.

ISBNs

Hardcover ISBN:979-8-88990-000-9

Paperback ISBN: 979-8-88990-004-7

E-book ISBN:979-8-88990-004-7

F-**First Edition**

Printed in the United States of America.

Book design, publishing imprint, and related materials by Trient Press®.

Table of Contents

Introduction

Welcome to the Age of Exposure

Today, everything is connected.

That sounds simple until you stop and think about what it actually means. Your email is connected to your bank. Your phone is connected to your identity. Your social media is connected to your reputation. Your cloud storage is connected to your documents. Your payroll, vendors, customers, calendar, contracts, taxes, insurance, photos, messages, and family communication all move through systems that were never designed with ordinary people in mind.

We built a world where convenience became the default. We wanted faster banking, faster messages, faster payments, faster sign-ins, faster customer service, faster everything. We got it. But we also created a world where every account, every app, every login, every profile, every vendor portal, every public post, and every connected device can become another doorway into our lives.

That is the age of exposure.

Exposure does not always mean your private information was stolen in some dramatic breach. Sometimes exposure is quieter than that. It is the phone number you posted publicly years ago. The email address tied to every account you own. The family photo that reveals more than you realized. The business filing that shows your address. The vendor portal nobody remembered to close. The social media account still connected to an old employee. The app on your phone that has access to your contacts, location, photos, camera, and microphone. The password you reused because you were tired and busy and had too many accounts to manage.

Exposure is the condition of being searchable, reachable, imitable, and vulnerable through the systems you use every day.

That is why cybersecurity cannot stay in the IT department anymore. It stopped being only about computers a long time ago. Cybersecurity is now about people. It is about businesses. It is about families. It is about money, identity, reputation, trust, payroll, vendors, social media, public records, phones, apps, and the decisions we make under pressure.

For years, many people were taught to think of cybersecurity as something technical. Something handled by someone in the back office. Something involving firewalls, antivirus software, servers, and complicated terminology. Those things still matter, but they are no longer the whole battlefield. The battlefield moved into the places where ordinary people live and work. It moved into email threads, text messages, fake invoices, social media profiles, phone calls, payroll changes, account recovery, cloud folders, QR codes, public posts, and voice messages that sound like someone we know.

This book is about that shift.

The invisible war is not invisible because nothing is happening. It is invisible because most people do not recognize the attack while it is happening. They see a message. They see an invoice. They see a job offer. They see a delivery notice. They see a fake investor. They see a bank alert. They see a password reset. They see a customer complaint. They see a profile with photos and a story. They see a voice that sounds familiar. They see something that looks normal enough to trust.

And that is the danger.

Modern cybercrime does not always look like a stranger breaking into a computer. Sometimes it looks like business. Sometimes it looks like opportunity. Sometimes it looks like customer service. Sometimes it looks like a family emergency. Sometimes it looks like a vendor update. Sometimes it looks like a professional email from a person you already know. Sometimes it looks like someone finally understands the vision you have been trying to build.

That last one matters to me personally.

I did not arrive at this subject as someone who only read about it from the outside. I have lived enough of it to understand how fast trust can become a weapon. Years ago, when I was trying to build my first company and searching for an angel investor, I did what a responsible founder is supposed to do. I used a reputable platform. I went through paperwork. I checked what I knew how to check. I thought I was talking to the right people. I thought I had found someone who understood the vision.

It still turned out to be a scam.

The damage was not only financial. It cost time. It cost momentum. It cost trust. It damaged reputation and confidence. It pulled energy away from building and forced it into recovery. And like many victims discover, the money and time do not magically return just because the criminals are eventually exposed. Even when people are arrested, even when lawsuits happen, even when everyone knows harm was done, the victim is often left rebuilding from the pieces.

That experience changed how I look at cybersecurity. It made me understand that ordinary people and business owners are being asked to defend themselves in a world where the rules are no longer obvious. Most owners do not have legal permission, technical access, investigative tools, or time to verify every IP address, trace every profile, inspect every domain, and prove every person is who they claim to be. Yet they are still expected to make decisions that can affect money, reputation, payroll, customers, and survival.

That is not a fair fight.

This book is not written for the person who already speaks fluent cybersecurity. It is written for the business owner who is tired of being told to buy another tool without understanding what problem it actually solves. It is written for the employee who gets an urgent message and does not know whether slowing down will get them in trouble. It is written for the parent trying to protect a family in a world of fake emergency calls and social media exposure. It is written for the founder chasing opportunity, the creator protecting a public identity, the professional who uses email all day, and the ordinary person who thinks cybersecurity is probably someone else's problem.

It is not someone else's problem anymore.

If you have an email address, you have a front door. If you have a phone, you may be carrying the master key. If you have social media, you have a public identity. If you run a business, you have money movement, vendors, customers, employee access, and reputation to protect. If you use apps, you have doorways. If you use one password everywhere, you have copied one key for multiple doors. If you post your life in real time, you are giving strangers a map. If you have old accounts you forgot about, those doors may still be open.

That does not mean you should live afraid. Fear is not the goal of this book. Clarity is.

I do not want readers to walk away paranoid. I want them to walk away awake. There is a difference. Paranoia makes you distrust everything and everyone. Awareness helps you understand which actions are risky, which doors matter, which requests need verification, which accounts deserve stronger protection, and which habits need to change. The point is not to stop living or stop doing business. The point is to stop being easy to process.

Cybercriminals do not always need to be brilliant. Sometimes they only need us to be exposed, rushed, trusting, tired, helpful, hopeful, embarrassed, or confused. They do not need every door to be open. They only need one. They do not need every employee to fail. They only need one rushed moment. They do not need every vendor to be compromised. They only need one convincing message. They do not need your whole identity at once. They can collect pieces over time.

That is why this book begins with exposure. Exposure is the foundation underneath the rest of the problem. Once people, businesses, tools, accounts, and records are exposed, criminals can study them. Once criminals can study them, they can impersonate them. Once they can impersonate them, they can manipulate trust. Once they can manipulate trust, they can move money, steal access, damage reputation, and create chaos.

The first part of this book explains the age we are living in. It shows why cybersecurity is no longer just an IT issue, why everyone is a target now, why the digital battlefield is everywhere, why exposure has become the new vulnerability, why small businesses are not too small to be attacked, and why cybercrime should be understood as an economy rather than a random collection of bad emails.

The second part looks at the attacks hiding in plain sight. Phishing does not look fake anymore. Email has become the front door. Passwords and phones have become keys to entire lives. Social engineering turns trust into an attack path. Ransomware and account takeovers are really about control. These are not abstract ideas. They are the things that happen every day to real people and real businesses.

The third part focuses on the human side. People do not get attacked because they are stupid. They get attacked because they are human. Smart people still get fooled because intelligence does not cancel out timing, emotion, hope, fear, pressure, or authority. Social media, public records, family members, employees, vendors, AI, deepfakes, and fake profiles all change the trust equation. In the age of exposure, trust is still necessary, but blind trust is dangerous.

The fourth part turns awareness into action. It explains the personal baseline every individual needs, the business baseline every company needs, why fewer tools mean fewer doors, why evidence and logs matter, why recovery must come after defense, and why every business now needs a real cybersecurity program.

The order matters.

We do not start with recovery and call that security. We start by closing doors. We reduce the number of ways criminals can get in. We control the keys. We verify what matters. We preserve proof. Then we build recovery for what still gets through. Something bad can still happen. That is reality. But recovery is not an excuse to leave the doors open. Recovery helps you restore control after good defense gets tested.

This is one of the strongest messages I want readers to carry through the entire book: cybersecurity is not about buying every tool. It is about operating differently. It is about knowing what you use, who has access, what matters most, what needs verification, what evidence exists, what doors can be closed, and what happens when something goes wrong.

A tool can help. A tool can warn you. A tool can manage passwords, protect devices, filter email, preserve evidence, or monitor risk. But a tool is not a strategy by itself. A business can have tools and still be wide open. A family can have apps and still be unprepared. A person can have antivirus and still share a code with a fake support caller. A company can have backups and still not know whether they work.

The future of cybersecurity is not more noise. It is more control.

That is also the philosophy behind the cybersecurity program I am building. The point is not to bury people under dashboards they do not understand. The point is to create a clearer way to see what matters, explain risk in plain English, preserve proof, guide response, reduce confusion, and help people act before damage spreads. The average person should not have to become a cybersecurity analyst just to know whether a message is dangerous, whether an account is exposed, or what to do next.

A strong system should help people answer simple but powerful questions. Am I safe enough today? What is open? Who has access? What changed? What needs verification? What proof do we have? What can be closed? What should happen next? Those are not just technical questions. They are life questions and business questions now.

This book will not tell you that you can eliminate every risk. That would be dishonest. It will not tell you that one product, one password, one app, one policy, or one person can solve the problem forever. That is not how the connected world works. The goal is not perfection. The goal is discipline. The goal is to become harder to trick, harder to impersonate, harder to rush, harder to use, harder to enter, and harder to keep compromised.

The goal is to protect what matters before someone else decides it has value.

For individuals, that means protecting email, phone, passwords, money, identity, social media, files, family, and recovery paths. For businesses, it means protecting money movement, employee access, vendors, payroll, customer records, domains, websites, social media, cloud files, evidence, and reputation. For public-facing people, it means understanding that identity itself can be targeted. For everyone, it means learning that verification is not rude, evidence is not paperwork, and recovery is not weakness. They are part of surviving the age we are in.

You may already have been exposed in ways you do not realize. Most of us have. That is not meant to shame you. It is meant to start the conversation from reality. Your email may be connected to old accounts. Your phone may be tied to recovery settings you forgot. Your information may appear on public sites. Your social media may reveal more than you intended. Your business may have tools nobody owns anymore. Your employees may have access that was never reviewed. Your vendors may be trusted without verification. Your family may not know what to do during a fake emergency.

The answer is not to panic. The answer is to begin.

Start with the obvious doors. Protect email. Protect the phone. Stop reusing important passwords. Turn on stronger authentication. Review who has access. Verify payment changes. Stop letting one message move money. Clean up old accounts. Reduce tools where possible. Preserve evidence before deleting. Build a recovery path after you have closed what you can. Teach people without shame. Make cybersecurity part of how life and business operate, not something you only think about after something goes wrong.

This is not a book about fear. It is a book about power. Not power in the dramatic sense. Practical power. The power to slow down when pressure appears. The power to verify before acting. The power to say no to confusion. The power to close a door you forgot was open. The power to protect an employee who reports quickly. The power to preserve proof. The power to recover with control instead of panic. The power to build a business that does not operate blind.

The invisible war is already here. It is in the inbox, the phone, the invoice, the profile, the cloud folder, the vendor request, the recovery code, the public post, the fake voice, and the business process no one thought to protect. But once you can see the battlefield, you can stop moving through it blindly.

Welcome to the age of exposure.

You do not need to become an expert overnight. But you do need to understand the world you are living in. You need to know where the doors are. You need to know who has the keys. You need to verify what matters. You need to preserve proof. You need to close what should not be open. You need to build the discipline to protect yourself, your family, your business, and your future.

Because in the age of exposure, the safest people are not the ones who pretend nothing can happen. They are the ones who see the doors, control the keys, and refuse to remain wide open.

Part I:

The World Changed — Most People Just Missed It

Chapter 1

The Day Everything Became Exposed

Today, everything became exposed.

Not because one company was breached. Not because one password was stolen. Not because one person clicked on one bad email. Those things matter, but they are only symptoms of something much bigger.

Everything became exposed because everything became connected.

Your email is connected to your phone. Your phone is connected to your bank. Your bank is connected to your identity. Your identity is connected to your social media. Your social media is connected to your family, your work, your habits, your travel, your reputation, and in many cases, your business. The files on your computer are not just files anymore. They are contracts, receipts, tax records, client information, photos, payroll records, and private conversations. Your phone is not just a phone. It is a command center for your entire life.

That is the part most people still have not accepted.

We are not living in a world where cybersecurity is only about someone trying to break into a computer and steal a file. That version of cybersecurity is too small for the world we live in now. Today, a criminal may not need to break into your computer at all. They may study your social media. They may pretend to be someone you know. They may send a message that looks normal, friendly, urgent, or professional. They may imitate a vendor, a friend, a family member, an employee, a client, or an investor. They may not need to force the door open, because too often, we open the door for them ourselves.

That is not meant as an insult. It is meant as a warning.

Cybersecurity is no longer just an IT problem. It is a life problem. It is a business problem. It is a reputation problem. It is a trust problem. It is a human problem.

For years, people treated cybersecurity like an optional expense. Something for banks. Something for government agencies. Something for big companies with technology departments. The average person would say, "I am not important enough to be hacked." The small business owner would say, "We are too small for anyone to care." The entrepreneur would say, "I will worry about security once I grow."

That thinking is outdated, and in some cases, dangerous.

If you think cybersecurity is just an IT thing, or you think you do not need it, or you believe it is only a gimmick to get you to pay for something you will never use, you may already have been touched by cybercrime. The real question is whether you know it yet.

That is the uncomfortable truth about the age of exposure. The attack does not always announce itself. Sometimes you do not hear alarms. Sometimes your screen does not go black. Sometimes no one calls and says, "You have been hacked." Sometimes your information is collected quietly, sold quietly, tested quietly, and used later when the timing is better for the criminal than it is for you.

By the time many people realize what happened, the damage is already moving through systems they cannot see.

But that does not mean people are powerless. It does not mean a business cannot recover. It does not mean there is no point in starting. It means the old mindset has to die.

It is never too late to start protecting yourself today.

I learned that lesson the hard way.

Years before I built a cybersecurity company, I was building another company. Like many founders, I was looking for capital. I was not careless. I was not throwing information into the wind. I was looking for an angel investor through what appeared to be reputable channels. This was around late 2018 into 2020, when I was pushing hard to move a business vision forward. I used a platform that was supposed to connect entrepreneurs with serious investors. I filled out the paperwork. I took the meetings. I followed the process. I did what responsible founders are told to do.

Eventually, I found someone who seemed to understand the vision.

That is one of the most dangerous parts of a good scam: it does not always look like a scam. Sometimes it looks like opportunity. Sometimes it looks like relief. Sometimes it looks like the one person who finally understands what you have been trying to build.

This person appeared legitimate. There were documents. There were websites. There were steps that looked official. There were ways to verify pieces of the story, and each piece seemed to make the next step feel reasonable. That is how sophisticated scams work. They do not always ask you to ignore every warning sign. They give you just enough proof to make the next request seem safe.

And still, it turned out to be a scam.

I want to be clear about what made that experience so important. It was not simply that someone lied. People lie every day. It was that the modern internet gave them enough tools to look credible, move quickly, hide behind distance, and exploit the limits of what an ordinary business owner can legally verify.

As a business owner, I could ask questions. I could review documents. I could search names. I could look at websites. I could check what was publicly available. But I did not have the legal authority or technical access to investigate every digital signal behind the scenes. I could not lawfully start tracing every IP address, verifying every building location, pulling network evidence, or proving whether a communication truly came from where it claimed to come from. That is not how the system works for ordinary people or ordinary companies.

And criminals know that.

They know most people do not have the tools. They know most small businesses do not have cyber investigators sitting in the office. They know founders are busy. They know entrepreneurs are hopeful. They know families are distracted. They know employees are moving fast. They know leaders want to trust people because business cannot happen without trust.

That is what makes this war invisible.

You are not always fighting a person you can see. You are fighting false identities, fake credibility, stolen information, copied language, social pressure, and technical hiding places. You may be dealing with people across the United States or in other countries. You may be one of many victims. You may do everything you believe is correct and still find yourself inside a machine designed to take your money, your time, your confidence, and your reputation.

In that case, there were arrests. There were legal proceedings. There were other victims. There was a broader pattern. But the money, the time, and the damage were not truly restored. That is another truth people need to understand: justice and recovery are not the same thing.

Someone can be arrested, and you can still lose years. Someone can be prosecuted, and your business can still be damaged. Someone can go to prison, and the money can still be gone.

People like to imagine that if a criminal is caught, everything goes back to normal. In real life, that is rarely how it feels. The business still has to recover. The reputation still has to be repaired. The opportunity may never return in the same form. The time is gone. The trust is changed.

That experience became one of the reasons I moved deeper into cybersecurity. Not because I wanted to live in fear. Not because I wanted to scare people. Because I understood, in a personal way, that the threat was no longer sitting only behind a firewall. It was sitting inside the way we communicate, the way we trust, the way we verify, and the way we expose ourselves every day.

Most cybercrimes do not begin the way people imagine. They do not always begin with a shadowy hacker breaking through a secure server. Many begin with a message. A post. A link. A fake profile. A familiar name. A password used too many times. A phone number placed in public. A family detail shared casually. A business relationship that was never verified beyond surface appearances.

They begin in ordinary life.

They happen on social media. They happen through phishing emails, scam emails, spam messages, fake invoices, fake stores, fake investment opportunities, fake job offers, fake delivery alerts, and fake people who sound real enough to earn a moment of trust. They happen when someone clicks because the message feels urgent or says, "I know this person," without stopping to verify whether the person on the screen is actually the person they know.

That is why exposure matters.

Exposure is everything you open up about your life, your business, your habits, and your systems. It is every doorway you create without realizing it is a doorway.

Look at your phone. If you have one hundred apps on it, you may have one hundred possible doorways into your life. Some are safer than others. Some are necessary. Some are well managed. Some are not. But every app asks for something. **Your location. Your contacts. Your camera. Your microphone. Your photos. Your email. Your payment information. Your login. Your behavior. Your attention.**

Now add your email accounts, social media accounts, cloud storage, banking apps, business tools, online shopping accounts, and old accounts you forgot existed. Add your employees, vendors, family members, assistants, contractors, and the people who have access to pieces of your life or business.

That is your real attack surface.

It is not just your computer. It is not just your office network. It is not just your files. It is the entire connected environment around you.

This is why cybersecurity has to move beyond the old conversation. A security program that only thinks about the files on your computer is not enough anymore. The files matter, but they are only one piece of the picture. Your identity, public information, passwords, habits, employees, family, vendors, phone, and recovery plan all matter.

And yes, I know what some people are thinking: "This sounds like too much. I cannot control all of that."

You are right. You cannot control everything.

Cybersecurity is not about controlling everything. It is about reducing unnecessary exposure, building better habits, creating stronger barriers, and knowing what to do when something goes wrong. It is about making yourself harder to fool, harder to impersonate, harder to exploit, and harder to destroy.

That is different from pretending you can make risk disappear.

Risk does not disappear. It gets managed.

I will also say something honest: I am not perfect at this. No serious cybersecurity professional should pretend they are. When I travel for an event, I may post about it. Sometimes I post from the event. Sometimes I wait until after.

Sometimes I am traveling by plane. Sometimes by car. Sometimes there is a photo. The difference is not that I never share. The difference is that I think about what I am sharing, when I am sharing it, who can see it, and what someone could do with it.

That is the difference between living online blindly and living online with awareness.

The goal is not to disappear from the world. For most of us, that is not realistic. We run businesses. We attend events. We speak publicly. We sell products. We build brands. We communicate with customers. We use social media because modern life and modern business require visibility.

The goal is not invisibility.

The goal is disciplined visibility.

You can be visible without being careless. You can be accessible without being exposed in every direction. You can build trust without handing strangers the keys to your life. You can use technology without treating every app, every message, and every platform as harmless.

For too long, cybersecurity has been discussed in a way that makes ordinary people feel either bored or helpless. The language sounds too technical. The tools feel too expensive. The warnings feel too dramatic. So people tune out. They assume the topic belongs to someone else.

But cybersecurity belongs to everyone now.

If you are a parent, a business owner, an employee, or an executive, it belongs to you. If you have a phone, an email address, a bank account, a social media profile, a cloud account, a client list, a family, a reputation, or a dream you are trying to build, it belongs to you.

The age of exposure does not care whether you consider yourself technical. Criminals do not only target people who understand cybersecurity. They target people who are busy, trusting, rushed, hopeful, distracted, overwhelmed, or convinced it will not happen to them.

That is why the old question, "Will I be attacked?" is the wrong question.

The better question is: when something happens, how fast will I notice, how much damage will it do, and how prepared will I be to recover?

That is not fear-based thinking. That is mature thinking.

We do this in other areas of life all the time. We wear seatbelts because crashes happen. We lock doors because access should be controlled. We buy insurance because risk exists. We keep records, sign contracts, check references, and ask for identification because trust works better when it has structure.

Cybersecurity is the same idea applied to the connected world.

Trust is not the enemy. Blind trust is.

Technology is not the enemy. Unprotected technology is.

Visibility is not the enemy. Undisciplined exposure is.

The internet made it easier to build, connect, sell, learn, speak, and grow. It also made it easier to copy, impersonate, manipulate, steal, and disappear. Both realities are true. If we celebrate the opportunity and ignore the risk, we leave ourselves open. If we fear the risk and ignore the opportunity, we stop building.

The answer is not panic. The answer is preparation.

That preparation begins with a simple admission: everything is connected.

Once you accept that, the way you look at your life changes. Your email is not just a mailbox. It is a recovery key for other accounts. Your phone number is not just a contact point. It may be tied to banking, verification codes, and identity checks. Your social media is not just entertainment. It may be a research file for someone trying to impersonate you or manipulate you. Your business website is not just marketing. It may reveal vendors, employees, services, locations, and operational clues. Your reused password is not just a bad habit. It may be the one key that opens five doors.

This is why exposure is the new vulnerability.

A vulnerability is not only a flaw in software. Sometimes, the vulnerability is the information you made available. Sometimes, it is the pattern you repeat. Sometimes, it is the assumption that the message must be real because it uses the right name. Sometimes, it is the fact that no one in the company knows who is allowed to approve payments, change payroll, access client files, or reset a password.

Cybersecurity is not simply about stopping criminals from breaking in. It is about reducing the number of ways they can convince us to let them in.

That is the war most people are missing.

It is quiet. It is constant. It is personal. It is professional. It follows us from our phones to our offices, from our inboxes to our bank accounts, from our social media to our families, from our private lives to our public reputations.

And because it is invisible, people underestimate it until it becomes visible through damage.

This book is not written to make you paranoid. Paranoia is not a strategy. Awareness is. Discipline is. Verification is. Recovery planning is. Stronger systems are. Better habits are. Clearer rules are.

If you walk away from this first chapter with one idea, let it be this: you do not need to become a cybersecurity expert to become harder to exploit.

You need to understand where you are exposed.

You need to stop treating convenience as if it has no cost.

You need to stop assuming that a familiar name on a screen means a familiar person is behind it.

You need to stop thinking small businesses, families, entrepreneurs, and ordinary professionals are beneath the attention of criminals.

And you need to build a security mindset that reaches beyond the files on your computer.

Because the invisible war did not begin when someone hacked you.

It began the moment your life, your business, and your trust became visible to people you never invited in.

Chapter 2

Cybersecurity Is No Longer an IT Problem

One of the biggest misconceptions in the modern world is that cybersecurity is an IT problem.

It is not.

It quit being only an IT problem a long time ago. In my view, that shift happened roughly twenty years ago, when the internet stopped being a place we visited and became a place we lived. The moment social media entered the picture, cybersecurity changed. The moment people began putting their names, faces, families, jobs, locations, opinions, purchases, relationships, and businesses online, the conversation changed.

Before that shift, many people thought of cybersecurity as protecting a computer. Protect the machine. Protect the network. Protect the files. Keep viruses out. Stop someone from breaking into a server. Make sure the company data stays locked away.

That was never the whole picture, but at least it made sense for the time.

Then the world moved.

Your identity moved online. Your relationships moved online. Your business operations moved online. Your banking moved online. Your payroll moved online. Your vendors moved online. Your client records moved online. Your marketing moved online. Your employees, customers, and partners began communicating through email, cloud platforms, websites, payment systems, phones, apps, and social media profiles.

At that point, cybersecurity stopped being about protecting only computers and became about protecting people.

That is the paradigm shift many companies still have not caught up with. Security is still too often treated as if it is sitting in a back room with a few technical people watching blinking lights on a screen. That picture is outdated. It may be comfortable because it allows everyone else to believe the problem belongs to someone else, but it is not reality.

Cybersecurity is an everyone problem now.

If you own a business, cybersecurity is your problem. If you work for a business, it is your problem. If you manage payroll, answer emails, post on social media, send invoices, approve payments, handle clients, travel with a laptop, use a personal phone for work, or log in to a cloud tool, it is your problem. If you are a parent, a professional, a contractor, a creator, an executive, or a student, it is your problem.

That does not mean everyone needs to become a technical expert. It means everyone has to understand that their behavior touches the security of the people and organizations around them.

This is where many businesses make their first serious mistake. They separate technology from operations. They say, "That is IT," as if IT is a locked room somewhere far away from payroll, banking, customers, employees, vendors, and leadership. But a modern business does not work that way. Every area of the business is connected.

Think about a normal day inside almost any company.

Payroll is online. Banking is online. Vendor payments are online. Client records are stored in digital systems. Employees use email. Teams use cloud tools. Sales may happen through a website or payment platform. Marketing happens through social media. Customer service happens through messages, portals, tickets, or inboxes. Documents are signed electronically. Files are shared through links. Meetings happen over video. Owners check accounts from phones. Employees work from home, from coffee shops, from airports, from hotels, from client sites, and sometimes from public Wi-Fi.

Show me the part of that business that has not been touched by the internet.

There is not much left.

That means cybersecurity is not sitting beside the business. It is running through the business. It is in the way money moves. It is in the way information is handled. It is in the way decisions are approved. It is in the way employees are trained. It is in the way customers are protected. It is in the way leaders communicate.

When a business owner misunderstands that, the danger becomes bigger than a technical inconvenience. A cyber incident can start as something that looks small and innocent, then turn into a chain reaction.

It may begin with an invoice.

An employee receives a message that appears to come from a real vendor. The logo looks familiar. The language sounds professional. The email says the vendor has changed banking information and future payments should go to a new account. The employee is busy. The business has paid this vendor before. Nothing about the request looks dramatic. It does not feel like a cyberattack. It feels like paperwork.

So the payment goes out.

Later, the real vendor calls and says, "We never changed our banking information. Where is the payment?"

Now what started as an email problem becomes a banking problem. The banking problem becomes a financial problem. The financial problem becomes a legal problem. The legal problem becomes a reputation problem. The reputation problem becomes a customer trust problem. And if the amount is large enough, or the company is already under pressure, that problem can become a survival problem.

That is why the phrase "IT problem" is so dangerous. It makes people look in the wrong direction.

The attack may not look technical at first. It may look like a normal request, a normal conversation, a normal login, a normal invoice, a normal message from someone you know, or a normal customer interaction. It may use technology, but the target is often judgment, trust, habit, pressure, or confusion.

In other words, the attacker may not need to hack your system if they can hack your process.

If they can convince an employee to send money, they have succeeded. If they can convince someone to give away a password, they have succeeded. If they can impersonate a client and collect sensitive information, they have succeeded. If they can pretend to be the owner and pressure someone into an urgent task, they have succeeded. If they can use a personal social media conversation to collect enough details to answer security questions, they have succeeded.

None of that fits neatly into the old idea of cybersecurity as only a device issue.

This is also why every employee is now part of the security system.

That statement makes some people uncomfortable because they hear blame in it. I do not mean it that way. Employees should not be treated like the enemy. They should not be shamed for not knowing things they were never taught. They should not be expected to carry the weight of company security without training, tools, policies, and support.

But we still have to be honest. If an employee touches one company system, they are part of the security system. If they open email, use a password, access client records, process payments, handle files, answer messages, or use a company device, their actions matter.

The solution is not to scare employees. The solution is to build security into the way the business works.

Too many companies make security harder than it needs to be. They have one portal for this, another app for that, another website for a separate task, another password for a different system, and no simple way for an employee to know what matters most. Then when something goes wrong, leadership acts surprised that people made decisions too quickly or skipped steps.

Security has to become more seamless. It has to be part of the daily flow of the business, not something bolted on after the damage is done. Clear approvals. Clear access. Clear training. Clear reporting. Clear rules for money movement. Clear rules for vendor changes. Clear rules for devices. Clear rules for employees who join the company and employees who leave.

Confusion is not a security strategy.

Personal habits also become business issues. This is another area where people do not always connect the dots.

Who are you talking to on Facebook? Do you actually know the person, or is it a fake profile? Can you prove it? How much information are you sharing in casual conversation? Are you using the same password across multiple accounts? Are you clicking links because you are busy and the message looks legitimate enough? Are you using your personal phone for business because it is convenient? Are you logging in from public Wi-Fi with a company laptop? Are you saving documents in the easiest place instead of the safest place? Are you sending files to yourself because the official system feels like too much work?

Really think about what you do every day.

Most people do not wake up planning to create risk. They are trying to get through the day. They are busy. They are tired. They are traveling. They are answering messages between meetings. They are trying to run payroll, make sales, respond to customers, care for family, and keep life moving. Cybercriminals know that. They count on it.

They do not need everyone to be careless all the time. They only need one person to be tired at the wrong moment. One person to click too fast. One person to reuse a password. One person to believe a fake profile. One person to approve a change without verifying it through a trusted channel.

That is why security culture matters.

The owner sets it. The CEO sets it. The founder sets it. The leader sets it. If leadership treats cybersecurity like an annoying expense, employees will treat it like an annoying expense. If leadership cuts corners, employees will cut corners. If leadership says, "Just get it done," without building a safe way to get it done, the business should not be surprised when people choose speed over protection.

But if leadership treats security as part of protecting the business, the culture changes. People learn to pause. They learn to verify. They learn that asking questions is not weakness. They learn that reporting something suspicious is not embarrassing. They learn that security is not there to slow the company down. It is there to keep the company alive.

This matters because the modern cyberattack is often built around impersonation.

Impersonation ties many of these threats together. Identity theft, social media scams, fake profiles, phishing, business email compromise, payment fraud, and fake vendor requests all live in the same neighborhood. The names may be different, but the game is the same: someone pretends to be someone they are not so they can get something they should not have.

Maybe they pretend to be a family member. Maybe they pretend to be a friend. Maybe they pretend to be your boss. Maybe they pretend to be a vendor, a bank, a client, a government office, a delivery company, a job recruiter, or a customer. The first goal may not be money. Sometimes the first goal is information.

That is where people underestimate casual conversation.

You think you are just chatting. You think it is harmless. You mention where you grew up, your mother's maiden name, your first car, your pet's name, your birthday, your school, your favorite team, your travel schedule, your children, your business plans, or the people you work with. To you, it is conversation. To someone else, it may be a file.

Some of that information can help someone impersonate you. Some of it can help them answer security questions. Some of it can help them guess passwords. Some of it can help them make a fake message sound real. Some of it can help them target your family, employees, or customers.

So when people ask whether social media scams are really cybersecurity issues, my answer is yes. When people ask whether impersonation is really cybersecurity, my answer is yes. When people ask whether identity theft belongs in this conversation, my answer is absolutely yes.

It is all connected.

That is the point.

A criminal who collects information through social media may use it for identity theft. A criminal who steals identity details may use them to get into accounts. A criminal who gets into accounts may use them to impersonate someone trusted. A criminal who impersonates someone trusted may use that access to steal money, data, reputation, or opportunity.

The lines people draw between these crimes are often administrative. In real life, they overlap.

This is why the average business owner is not ignoring cybersecurity because they are foolish. Many simply do not understand what needs to be done before something goes wrong. That difference matters. If we frame every victim as careless, people stop listening. They become defensive. They hide mistakes. They avoid reporting suspicious activity because they do not want to look stupid.

That helps the criminal.

The better approach is to recognize that most people were never trained for the world they are now operating in. They were handed phones, apps, cloud platforms, payment portals, social media accounts, remote work tools, and digital banking, but they were not handed a practical security education to match.

So they improvise.

They use the same password because it is easier to remember. They click the link because the email looks professional. They send the file because the client is waiting. They approve the change because the vendor sounds impatient. They post from the airport because they are excited about the event. They log in from public Wi-Fi because work needs to get done. They assume the profile is real because the photo looks real.

This is not a character flaw. It is a training gap.

But criminals exploit gaps whether we meant to create them or not.

To the business owner who says, "I am too small to need cybersecurity," I would ask a simple question: do you have clients?

If the answer is yes, you are not too small.

Do you have one employee?

Then you are not too small.

Do you use email? Accept payments? Store records? Pay vendors? Use payroll? Manage passwords? Communicate with customers? Have a website? Use social media? Keep files on a computer? Use a phone to access accounts?

Then you are not too small.

Being small does not make you invisible. In some cases, it makes you easier. A small business may have fewer controls, less training, weaker processes, shared passwords, no dedicated security staff, and no clear recovery plan. That does not mean the business is bad. It means it is exposed.

And exposure is what attackers look for.

A small business owner may say, "No one would waste time on us." But the criminal may not be looking at you personally. They may be using automation. They may be sending the same scam to thousands of businesses. They may be testing passwords stolen from another breach. They may be looking for any company that will click, pay, respond, or panic.

The attack does not need to be personal to hurt you personally.

That is what people need to understand.

Cybersecurity also protects reputation and customer trust. This part does not get enough attention. When a business loses money, that is painful. When a business loses files, that is painful. But when a business loses trust, the damage can last much longer.

Customers want to believe you are careful with their information. Employees want to believe their payroll and personal data are safe. Vendors want to know they are dealing with the real company. Partners want to know your systems will not become a problem for them. If something goes wrong, people do not only ask, "Were they attacked?" They ask, "Were they prepared? Did they take this seriously? Can I still trust them?"

That is why cybersecurity is leadership.

It is not just software. It is not just hardware. It is not just an IT ticket. It is how an organization protects what matters most. Money matters. Files matter. Systems matter. But behind all of that are people: customers, employees, families, founders, partners, and communities.

Cybersecurity is about protecting them.

That is why this book will keep coming back to a broader definition of security. If your program only protects the files on a computer, it is not enough for the world we live in now. Your security has to include identity, reputation, communication, trust, payments, vendors, devices, social media behavior, employee access, recovery planning, and leadership culture.

This does not mean every person or small business needs the same system as a government agency or a Fortune 500 company. It means everyone needs a baseline. Everyone needs awareness. Everyone needs better habits. Everyone needs to know what to verify, what to protect, what to report, and what to do when something feels wrong.

Security is not only for the wealthy. It is not only for large corporations. It is not only for technical people. It is not only for people who already know they are under attack.

Cybersecurity is meant for everyone.

It does not matter what your income level is. It does not matter how many employees you have. It does not matter whether you work from a corporate office, a home office, a truck, a salon, a restaurant, a studio, a classroom, or a laptop at your kitchen table. If your life touches the internet, your life touches cybersecurity.

And if your business touches people, money, records, devices, communication, or trust, your business touches cybersecurity.

The question is not whether you are technical enough to care.

The question is whether you are connected enough to be exposed.

And today, almost everyone is.

So we have to stop saying, "That is IT's problem."

It is not.

It is the owner's problem. It is the employee's problem. It is the customer's problem. It is the family's problem. It is the leader's problem. It is the community's problem. It belongs to everyone who participates in a connected world.

Cybersecurity is no longer the job of one department. It is the responsibility of every person, every device, every password, every payment, every message, and every decision connected to your life or business.

At the center of all of it is one truth: cybersecurity is not only about protecting technology anymore.

It is about protecting what matters most.

And what matters most is you.

Chapter 3

Why Everyone Is a Target Now

The question I hear all the time is simple: "Why would anyone target me?"

My honest answer is this: most of the time, they are not targeting you in the way you think they are.

They may not know your name. They may not know your business. They may not know your family, your income, your career, or what you are trying to build. They may not have woken up that morning and decided, "Today I am going after this one person."

That is not always how modern cybercrime works.

Many times, they are targeting the apps you use. They are targeting the platforms you trust. They are targeting the weak process, the exposed account, the reused password, the public profile, the business email, the payment system, the cloud tool, the fake vendor request, the fake customer message, or the login page that looks close enough to the real thing.

Once they get into the app, the account, the platform, or the system, you become part of their inventory.

You become another name. Another login. Another contact list. Another payment method. Another inbox. Another identity. Another opportunity.

That is why the old idea of being "important enough" to be targeted is so misleading. You do not have to be famous. You do not have to be wealthy. You do not have to be a celebrity, a CEO, a government official, or a major corporation. In many cases, being ordinary makes you easier.

That sounds harsh, but it is true.

It is often easier to wipe out a person who does not have a security team than it is to attack a person surrounded by lawyers, investigators, corporate controls, public visibility, and technical defenses. It is often easier to exploit a small business that has three people trying to do twenty jobs than it is to go after a large company with departments, monitoring, insurance, incident response plans, and dedicated staff.

Criminals understand effort. They understand return. They understand weakness. They understand volume.

They are not always looking for the biggest fish. They are often looking for the easiest catch.

That is the part people miss.

Most ordinary people are valuable to cybercriminals because they are easy. Not because they are foolish. Not because they deserve it. Not because they are careless in every part of life. They are valuable because they were never taught how this world works, and they are moving through a digital environment that was built faster than most people could learn to defend themselves inside it.

You were given apps before you were given security education. You were given social media before you were given verification habits. You were given online banking before you were given fraud awareness. You were given cloud storage before you were given access control. You were given convenience before anyone explained the cost.

That makes people vulnerable.

Small businesses are in the same position, only with more pressure.

A small business owner is trying to make payroll, serve clients, pay vendors, answer emails, sell products, manage employees, watch cash flow, handle taxes, keep customers happy, and still grow. Then we tell that person, "You also need cybersecurity." The owner already has too many tools, too many bills, too many platforms, too many passwords, too many logins, and not enough time.

Under normal circumstances, the tools they need may feel too expensive. If the tools are affordable, they may not know which ones matter. If they already have tools, they may be overwhelmed by them. They may not want to add another portal, another dashboard, another training system, another password policy, another app, another subscription, or another thing they have to manage.

It gets messy.

Cybercriminals benefit from messy.

They benefit when the owner is overwhelmed. They benefit when no one knows who is responsible. They benefit when passwords are shared. They benefit when invoices are approved too quickly. They benefit when a former employee still has access. They benefit when vendor changes are not verified. They benefit when the business is too busy to slow down.

This is why small businesses are attractive targets. Not because every small business has millions of dollars sitting in the bank, but because many small businesses have real money, real clients, real data, real reputation, and weak protection around all of it.

A criminal does not have to destroy the largest company in the world to make money. They can hit small companies over and over again. They can attack the same type of weakness repeatedly. They can send the same message to hundreds or thousands of people. They can test stolen passwords against many sites. They can clone a business page. They can pretend to be a vendor. They can create a fake invoice. They can send a fake job offer. They can build a fake customer complaint. They can impersonate a real person and wait for one victim to respond.

This is where automation changed the game.

The criminal does not need to know you personally. They need to know the pattern. They need to know the platform. They need to know the algorithm. They need to know what people click, what people trust, what people ignore, and what people are too busy to verify.

In the world of artificial intelligence, that problem gets bigger. A criminal can create more messages, more fake profiles, more believable wording, more targeted scams, and more variations than one person could have managed by hand in the past. They can move faster. They can test more angles. They can imitate tone. They can make a message sound professional. They can make a fake business look polished. They can create the feeling of legitimacy at scale.

And as computing power grows, as automation improves, and as new technologies enter the field, the pressure will only increase. Whether we are talking about AI today or quantum computing in the future, the direction is obvious: attacks become faster, more scalable, and harder for the average person to recognize without better systems and better habits.

That is why the target is no longer just the person.

The target is the connection.

The target is the account. The app. The password. The trust relationship. The habit. The public information. The business process. The moment of distraction. The system everyone depends on but no one questions until it breaks.

For regular people, the first thing criminals often want is identity. Before they can take over your life, they need pieces of you. They need passwords. They need access to your email. They need bank access. They want contacts, photos, tax records, medical insurance information, addresses, dates of birth, family connections, and anything that helps them look more like you or understand how to pressure you.

People sometimes underestimate the value of ordinary information. They think, "Who cares about my contacts? Who cares about my photos? Who cares about an old tax document? Who cares about my insurance card?"

Criminals care.

Your contacts can become their next victims. Your photos can be used to create trust or impersonate you. Your tax records may contain personal details that are difficult to change. Your medical or insurance information can be used for fraud. Your email can unlock other accounts. Your phone number may be tied to verification. Your old password may still open a forgotten account. Your address and family details may help someone sound legitimate.

Identity theft is not always one dramatic act. Sometimes it is built piece by piece.

That is what makes it dangerous.

For small businesses, the list changes but the logic stays the same. Criminals want banking. They want payment access. They want client lists. They want employee information. They want invoices. They want tax records. They want vendor relationships. They want your address. They want your logo. They want to know how your business communicates and how your customers recognize you.

Why?

Because if they can duplicate enough of your business online, they can steal from people while wearing your face.

They can create a fake page that looks like you. They can send messages that sound like you. They can run ads that use your name. They can contact your clients. They can collect payments. They can harvest information. They can damage your reputation and then disappear, leaving you to explain why customers were hurt by something you did not do.

You become the scapegoat.

This is where cybercrime becomes more than a technology issue. It becomes a brand issue. It becomes a legal issue. It becomes a trust issue. It becomes a survival issue.

Imagine a small business with a good local reputation. A fake account appears using the business name and logo. Customers receive messages about a special discount or urgent account update. The link goes to a page that looks close enough to be believable. Some customers enter personal information. Some make payments. Then the complaints start coming in.

The customers do not begin by blaming an unknown criminal. They blame the name they recognize.

Your name.

Or imagine a fake invoice that appears to come from a vendor your company uses. The invoice is formatted well. It includes language that sounds normal. It asks for payment to a new account. Someone pays it. By the time the real vendor follows up, the money is gone and the relationship is damaged.

Or imagine a fake job offer posted under the name of a real company. Applicants submit resumes, identification, banking details for direct deposit, or copies of personal documents. The company never posted the job, but victims believe they were dealing with that company. Now the company has to deal with the fallout.

These examples are not science fiction. They are demonstrations of how ordinary trust can be weaponized.

Social media made this easier.

Social media has become one of the great gathering places of modern life. It can connect people, build brands, promote events, share ideas, and give small businesses visibility they never could have afforded in the past. I am not against social media. Used well, it is powerful.

But we also have to be honest about what it created.

It created the playground where cybercrime could grow.

People put their lives online. Businesses put their teams online. Families put their relationships online. Leaders put their travel online. Employees list their job titles online. Vendors interact in public. Customers complain in public. Everyone becomes easier to study.

A criminal does not need to break into your house to learn about you if you publish the blueprint of your life every day.

They can learn who you know. They can learn where you work. They can learn what events you attend. They can learn what you complain about. They can learn who your children are, who your employees are, who your vendors are, and what your business is trying to do. They can see when you are traveling. They can see when you are distracted. They can see what you value.

Then they can use that information to make the next message feel real.

That is the power of social engineering. The scam does not have to be perfect. It only has to be believable at the right moment.

We have also become too compliant as a society. We click accept. We agree to terms we do not read. We answer questions because a screen asks us to. We enter information because a form looks official. We respond to messages because someone uses a familiar name. We send documents because the request sounds urgent. We trust platforms because everyone else uses them.

That compliance makes people valuable.

It also makes their networks valuable.

Think about your contacts. Use a simple number. Say you have one hundred contacts connected to you through your phone, email, social media, or business life. Out of that hundred, how many do you know deeply? Maybe the top ten percent. Maybe fewer. You might know where a few people live, where they bank, who their family is, how they write, how they speak, and what is normal for them. But most of the people in your digital life sit in the background. You recognize the name. You may not know much more.

That is enough for a criminal.

They do not need everyone in your network to fall for the scam. They only need one person to become the fish on the hook.

If they compromise one account, they can message the contacts. If they create one fake profile, they can build trust with people who assume the name is familiar. If they get into one business inbox, they can study conversations and time their request. If they find one weak link in the chain, they can use that link to reach others.

Your family can become a pathway to you. Your employees can become a pathway to the business. Your vendors can become a pathway to your money. Your clients can become a pathway to your reputation. Your friends can become a pathway to your identity.

That is not paranoia. That is how connected systems work.

When everything is connected, no one stands completely alone.

This is also why end-to-end encryption, while important, does not solve the whole problem. Encryption can protect a message while it travels from one point to another. That matters. But encryption does not stop someone from voluntarily sharing sensitive information with the wrong person. It does not stop a fake profile from building trust. It does not stop a compromised device from exposing what happens at the endpoint. It does not stop a person from clicking a fake link. It does not stop a business from paying a fake invoice.

Security is not only about whether the message is protected in transit.

It is also about who is on the other side, what you are sharing, what system you are using, what information is already exposed, and what happens after the message arrives.

You are only as secure as the apps you use, the people you trust, the habits you repeat, and the systems you depend on.

That does not mean you should stop using technology. It means you should stop assuming technology is safe simply because it is familiar.

Cybercrime can happen to anyone, at any time, in any place. It can happen because your own password was weak. It can happen because your bank was breached. It can happen because a government agency, a healthcare provider, a school, a vendor, a payment processor, or a platform you use was compromised. It can happen because someone close to you was hacked. It can happen because a criminal used information you never realized was public.

That is one of the most frustrating parts of the age of exposure. You can make better choices and still be affected by someone else's weak security. Your life is connected to institutions, businesses, platforms, and people you do not control.

This is why the individual blame game does not work.

Yes, personal responsibility matters. Yes, businesses must do better. Yes, employees need training. Yes, people need stronger habits. But we also have to recognize that the modern person lives inside a network of systems. Your risk is not limited to what you personally touch. It also includes what touches you.

So what do we do?

We stop pretending that only important people get targeted.

We stop pretending that small businesses are too small.

We stop pretending that social media is harmless.

We stop pretending that a password is just a password, an app is just an app, a contact is just a contact, or a message is just a message.

We start looking at exposure the way criminals look at exposure: as opportunity.

That shift is not meant to make life heavier. It is meant to make people stronger. When you understand that criminals are often looking for easy targets, you can make yourself harder to exploit. When you understand that they use automation, you can stop taking every attack personally and start building better defenses. When you understand that your network can be used against you, you can verify more carefully. When you understand that your business name can be copied, you can monitor and protect it more seriously.

You do not have to live in fear.

You do have to live awake.

Everyone is a target now because everyone is connected now. That is the new reality. The target may be your password, your app, your business page, your invoice process, your contact list, your vendor, your child, your employee, your customer, your phone, or your trust.

It may not begin with you.

But it can still end at your door.

You do not have to be famous, wealthy, powerful, or careless to become a target. In the age of exposure, being connected is enough.

Chapter 4

The New Digital Battlefield

The digital battlefield has been around longer than most people realize.

We talk about cybercrime as if it suddenly appeared when everyone got a smartphone, but the truth is that the battlefield was forming decades ago. It was forming when computers moved from specialized rooms into offices. It was forming when businesses started depending on networks. It was forming when email became normal. It was forming when payment systems, records, documents, and communications began moving into digital spaces.

In many ways, this battlefield has been with us since the 1980s. We just did not recognize it for what it was.

That is understandable. Most people were taught to think of battlefields as physical places. We think of land. Borders. Trenches. Bases. Uniforms. Weapons. Maps. Command centers. We think of history books, generals, tanks, ships, planes, and soldiers moving across visible territory.

The new battlefield does not look like that.

It does not always have smoke. It does not always have noise. It does not always have a front line you can point to on a map. There may be no uniform, no face, no warning, no visible enemy standing across from you.

The new battlefield is your phone. Your email. Your social media. Your apps. Your business software. Your cloud storage. Your payment systems. Your online accounts. Your customer records. Your vendor relationships. Your login credentials. Your digital footprint.

Anything that uses a computer interface can become part of it.

Your bank app is part of it. Your payroll system is part of it. Your PlayStation account can be part of it. Your smart TV, your tablet, your laptop, your work portal, your online store, your delivery app, your tax software, your customer database, and the old account you forgot you still had can all become part of the battlefield.

That is hard for the average person to absorb because the battlefield does not feel like a battlefield. It feels like daily life. You wake up, check your phone, open your email, respond to messages, pay a bill, check a bank balance, approve an invoice, upload a file, scroll social media, use a business app, and move on. Nothing about that feels like combat.

But from a criminal's point of view, each of those actions may create a point of attack.

That is why we have to update the way we think.

Old-school cybersecurity made people think the goal was to protect the computer. Keep the virus out. Keep someone from getting into the machine. Keep embarrassing photos from being stolen. Keep files from being copied. Protect the network from the hacker trying to break through the wall.

That world still exists, but it is not enough anymore.

The modern threat is not only about someone stealing an embarrassing photo off your phone. It is about someone hunting down your identity. It is about someone finding the small pieces of your life that can be used to get closer to your money, your business, your accounts, your clients, your family, or your reputation.

They may start with a phone number. They may start with a credit card attached to a phone. They may start with a gaming account, a shopping account, a social media account, or an email address connected to everything else. They may start with one old password you reused years ago. They may start with a business tool that no one monitors carefully. They may start with a message that looks harmless enough to click.

The first move may look small.

That does not mean the damage stays small.

Traditional war is fought over territory. Cyberwar is often fought over access.

Traditional war tries to control land, supply lines, and physical movement. Cybercrime tries to control accounts, systems, identities, money, and trust. Traditional war often announces itself. Cybercrime often hides until the attacker has what they came for. Traditional war depends on visible force. Cybercrime often depends on invisible permission.

That is the part people need to understand. In the digital world, attackers may not need to overpower you. They may only need to persuade you. They may not need to break the wall. They may only need you, an employee, a vendor, a client, or a family member to open the door.

This is not about turning every reader into a military strategist. You do not need to be General Patton to protect yourself in the digital age. You do not need to command an army, read technical reports all day, or understand every line of code behind the tools you use.

But you do need to understand where you are standing.

You are standing on a battlefield every day, whether you call it that or not.

One of the reasons people miss this is because cybersecurity has become too complicated in the public imagination. For the average person, it can feel like you almost need a PhD to understand it. There are acronyms, compliance standards, technical products, threat reports, insurance terms, legal terms, and software categories that change every year. The language alone can make people shut down.

That is a problem.

If the average person cannot understand the threat, the average person cannot defend against it. If a small business owner cannot understand what matters, they will either ignore security or buy the wrong things. If employees cannot understand the rules, they will break them by accident. If families cannot understand exposure, they will keep oversharing and wondering why scams feel so personal.

So let us make this plain.

The battlefield is wherever your life or business connects to technology.

That means your phone may be the most important battlefield you carry.

Your phone is not just a communication device. It is a gateway into your personal life and, for many people, into your business life. It holds email, banking, photos, contacts, calendars, social media, work apps, authentication codes, location history, text messages, payment apps, travel information, health apps, and sometimes access to company systems.

How many apps are on your phone right now?

Ten? Fifty? One hundred? More?

Each one may be useful. Each one may also be a doorway. Some doorways are locked better than others. Some are managed by serious companies. Some are not. Some ask for more access than they should. Some store data you forgot you gave them. Some connect to accounts that connect to other accounts.

That is why the phone matters so much. If your phone becomes compromised, stolen, cloned, unlocked, or manipulated through a scam, the attacker may not just have a device. They may have a map of your life.

This is also why business owners have to pay attention to tool sprawl.

Modern companies use too many disconnected tools. One app for payroll. Another for banking. Another for invoices. Another for marketing. Another for social media. Another for customer records. Another for scheduling. Another for documents. Another for employee communication. Another for accounting. Another for project management. Another for online signatures.

Each tool may solve a problem. But each tool also opens a new doorway into the company.

That does not mean every tool is bad. A well-run business needs technology. The problem is when the tools are disconnected, unmanaged, poorly understood, or added without a security plan. The problem is when no one knows who has access. The problem is when a former employee still has a login. The problem is when vendors can enter systems no one reviews. The problem is when the owner does not know which platforms hold sensitive data. The problem is when everyone assumes someone else is watching the doors.

A business does not become safer because it has more tools.

A business becomes safer when it knows what tools it uses, why it uses them, who can access them, what data they hold, and how quickly the business can lock them down when something goes wrong.

The weakest points on the modern digital battlefield are often not the most technical points. They are the points of confusion. The handoffs. The approvals. The shared accounts. The personal devices used for company work. The vendor requests. The unknown apps. The old systems no one removed. The employee who never received training. The owner who is too busy to verify before approving a payment.

That is where criminals move.

They move through the gaps between tools. They move through the gaps between people. They move through the gaps between what a company thinks is happening and what is actually happening.

Employees can become entry points. Vendors can become entry points. Clients can become entry points. Family members can become entry points. Again, that does not mean those people are enemies. It means attackers understand relationships. They understand that people trust people they know, or think they know. They understand that a message from a familiar name gets treated differently than a message from a stranger.

If a criminal cannot get directly to the owner, they may try an employee. If they cannot get to the employee, they may try a vendor. If they cannot get to the vendor, they may try a family member. If they cannot break the business system, they may try the personal account connected to the person who has access to the business system.

The battlefield surrounds the target.

That is why cybersecurity cannot stay trapped inside the old idea of a firewall around one office. People work from everywhere now. Information moves everywhere. Trust relationships move everywhere. A company may have no traditional office at all and still have dozens of digital doorways.

Artificial intelligence has changed this battlefield even more.

It is no longer just one person sitting behind a keyboard trying to attack one person they already know or one company they already researched by hand. AI allows criminals to scale. They can create better messages. They can write cleaner emails. They can imitate business language. They can generate fake customer complaints, fake vendor updates, fake job postings, fake investment opportunities, and fake documents that look professional enough to pass a quick glance.

They can create fake people.

They can create fake business pages.

They can clone the feeling of a legitimate company and route everything to an account they control.

The quality of deception has improved. That matters because many people still rely on old warning signs. They look for misspelled words, awkward grammar, strange formatting, or messages that obviously do not sound right. Those signs still matter when they appear, but they are no longer enough. A scam can now be polished. It can sound educated. It can sound corporate. It can sound local. It can sound like someone who understands your industry.

Voice is changing too. Deepfake audio and synthetic voices are making it harder to trust what we hear. A voice message may sound like someone you know. A video may look believable enough to create pressure. A document may appear official enough to move someone into action. A business page may look real enough to collect payments before anyone realizes it is a copy.

This does not mean every voice, video, or document is fake. It means verification matters more than ever.

Speed also matters.

Scammers have gotten faster. Automated attacks can move quickly. Fake pages can appear quickly. Messages can spread quickly. A compromised account can be used to contact many people before the real owner understands what happened. A payment can move out of reach before the business knows it was sent to the wrong place.

Reporting is often slower than the attack. Recovery is often slower than the damage. The victim may not know who the scammer is, where they are, what infrastructure they used, or which account they control. By the time the business starts asking questions, the criminal may already be gone.

That is one of the realities of the new battlefield: the attacker often moves faster than the victim can recognize, report, or recover.

So prevention and preparation matter.

A leader or business owner who understands this should do something very practical: downsize and organize the doorways.

Minimize how many tools you use where you can. Consolidate systems when it makes sense. Remove old accounts. Review who has access. Separate personal and business devices when possible. Do not let every new convenience become another unguarded entrance. Do not keep adding tools just because they are popular. Ask what data they hold. Ask who controls them. Ask what happens if the account is compromised. Ask how quickly you can revoke access.

You do not need to make your business primitive. You need to make it intentional.

There is a difference.

A modern business can use technology and still be disciplined. A person can use a smartphone and still be aware. A leader can use cloud tools and still insist on access control. A family can use social media and still think before sharing details that make them easier to target.

The goal is not to leave the battlefield. In the modern world, that is nearly impossible. The goal is to stop walking across it blindfolded.

This is where the message becomes hopeful.

Yes, you are on a battlefield. But you do not need to be a general. You do not need to master every technical detail. You do not need to panic every time your phone buzzes. You do not need to throw away every app, delete every account, or live disconnected from the world.

There is a better way.

You start by knowing what you use. You reduce what you do not need. You protect what matters most. You verify before trusting. You slow down before sending money or information. You train your employees. You separate personal convenience from business risk. You make recovery part of the plan before something happens.

That is not fear. That is maturity.

The new battlefield is not somewhere far away. It is in your pocket, your inbox, your business, your bank account, your reputation, and every system you trust without questioning.

The sooner you understand that, the sooner you can stop being an easy target and start becoming a harder one.

Chapter 5

Exposure Is the New Vulnerability

For a long time, when people heard the word vulnerability, they thought about technology.

An outdated program. A weak password. A missing software update. A server that was not patched. A firewall rule someone forgot to configure. A bug in an application that allowed the wrong person to get in.

Those vulnerabilities still matter. They always will. But they are no longer the whole story.

In the modern world, exposure is the new vulnerability.

That means the weakness is not always hidden inside a piece of software. Sometimes the weakness is sitting in public. Sometimes it is sitting on your phone. Sometimes it is in your social media posts, your business tools, your vendor relationships, your old accounts, your personal habits, your public records, your employee directory, or the way your company moves money.

Sometimes the vulnerability is not something broken.

Sometimes the vulnerability is something revealed.

That is the part people need to understand. We have gained enormous freedom in the digital world. We can run businesses from phones. We can work from almost anywhere. We can speak to clients across the country. We can store files in the cloud, sign contracts electronically, move money instantly, market to strangers, hire remotely, and build reputations without needing a physical storefront.

That freedom is powerful. It is also expensive.

The price of that freedom is exposure.

Every account, every app, every platform, every profile, every integration, every public post, and every connected service creates another possible doorway. Some of those doors are necessary. Some are helpful. Some are locked well. Some are not. But they are still doors.

Think of exposure as a weakness that can be exploited.

In ordinary life, if someone knows a person's weakness, they can use it. If they know a person is desperate to be liked, they can flatter them. If they know a person is afraid of disappointing others, they can pressure them into helping. If they know a person has a habit, a craving, an insecurity, a fear, or a blind spot, they can aim directly at that spot.

The internet did not invent exploitation. It scaled it.

Today, the weakness may not be a cigarette, a drink, a fear, or an insecurity. It may be the need to be helpful. It may be the desire to respond quickly. It may be the habit of clicking before thinking. It may be the belief that a familiar logo means a trustworthy message. It may be the fact that your email address, phone number, family details, company name, job title, and public schedule are all available in different places for someone to collect.

That is what makes modern exposure so dangerous. It does not always look like risk when it is happening.

A person posts a family photo. A business announces a new employee. A founder thanks a vendor. A leader posts from an event. A company shares a screenshot of a dashboard. An employee lists a job title online. A small business owner uses the same email for banking, payroll, cloud tools, vendors, and social media.

Each action may seem normal.

But to someone building a profile, normal information becomes useful information.

This is where old-school cybersecurity and modern exposure separate.

An old-school vulnerability might be outdated software. A modern exposure might be your phone number in the wrong place. It might be your business email format. It might be a staff list on your website. It might be a post that tells people you are traveling. It might be a public complaint that reveals which vendor you use. It might be a photo that shows a badge, a computer screen, a client name, a whiteboard, a license plate, a school name, or an office layout.

An old-school vulnerability may require a technical exploit.

A modern exposure may only require attention.

A criminal does not always need to break into the system first. Sometimes they can study the people around the system. They can study what is public. They can study who has authority. They can study how your company communicates. They can study the language you use, the events you attend, the tools you mention, the vendors you thank, and the people who work with you.

Then they use that information to make the attack feel normal.

That is the modern threat.

It is not always a stranger shouting from the outside. It is often a stranger who has learned enough to sound familiar.

This is why I say exposure is the new vulnerability. The danger is not only what hackers can break into. The danger is what we have already placed in front of them.

Most people give up more than they realize.

Names. Birthdays. Phone numbers. Email addresses. Family members. Children. Spouses. Travel plans. Business partners. Vendors. Employee names. Job titles. Client relationships. Screenshots. Receipts. License plates. Home addresses. Office locations. Security-question answers. Old usernames. Old accounts. Favorite teams. Pet names. School names. Childhood details. Places of birth. Photos of documents. Photos of badges. Photos of events.

Individually, those details may feel small.

Together, they become a map.

A criminal does not need every detail. They need enough details to make the next move easier. Enough to answer a question. Enough to reset an account. Enough to sound like you. Enough to impersonate someone you know. Enough to make a bank, vendor, employee, or customer believe the request is legitimate.

People often think of identity theft as someone stealing a Social Security number and opening an account. That happens. But identity theft can also begin with softer information. The kind of information people casually reveal every day.

Where did you grow up? What school did you attend? What was your first car? What is your mother's maiden name? What is your pet's name? What city were you born in? What is your favorite team? What is your child's birthday? What events do you attend? Who do you trust? Who handles your payroll? Who works in your office? Who is your assistant? Who approves payments?

Some of those questions sound like conversation.

Some sound like security questions.

That is the point.

In a world where institutions still use personal history to verify identity, oversharing becomes more than a privacy issue. It becomes an access issue.

The same thing happens in business.

Business owners expose more than they realize, and not only through what they intentionally post. A company may expose its software stack through job listings, employee profiles, email signatures, browser screenshots, support pages, login portals, integrations, public reviews, help-wanted ads, and casual social media posts.

A business owner may not think they are revealing anything sensitive. But the business may be telling the world which payroll provider it uses, which customer system it uses, what accounting platform it uses, what cloud tools it depends on, who handles operations, who manages finance, who the vendors are, who the clients are, and when the office is open or closed.

The risk is not always one dramatic leak.

Often, it is too many small windows.

Too many tabs. Too many browsers. Too many dashboards. Too many tools. Too many disconnected systems. Too many places where information gets lost. Too many people with access. Too many apps connected to other apps. Too many accounts that no one reviews.

A business can be exposed by its own complexity.

That is one of the biggest problems in small and mid-sized organizations today. Leaders keep adding tools to solve problems, but every tool creates another relationship, another login, another permission, another vendor, and another place where something can go wrong. Over time, the company becomes harder to defend because no one has a clear picture of what is connected to what.

That is not strategy.

That is digital clutter with consequences.

Criminals understand clutter. They understand that a scattered business has blind spots. They understand that the finance tool may not talk to the HR tool. They understand that the owner may not know which employees still have access. They understand that a vendor change may happen by email because there is no controlled approval system. They understand that an old account may still be active because no one remembers creating it.

Exposure grows in the gaps between what a company uses and what a company actually controls.

Now go into the mind of the criminal for a moment.

A criminal does not always begin by attacking. Many begin by collecting.

They search. They watch. They scrape. They study. They compare details from different places. They look at your social media. They look at your company website. They look at public records. They look at business registrations. They look at data broker sites. They look at employee profiles. They look at vendor mentions. They look at reviews. They look at job posts. They look at old leaks. They look at email patterns.

They are building a profile.

Not always by hand. Sometimes with automation. Sometimes with tools that gather information quickly. Sometimes with artificial intelligence helping them organize what they found and turn it into messages, fake profiles, fake documents, or fake requests.

Once the profile is strong enough, the attack becomes easier.

If they know your role, they can target your authority.

If they know your vendors, they can fake a vendor message.

If they know your employees, they can impersonate internal communication.

If they know your family details, they can create urgency.

If they know your travel schedule, they can time the attack.

If they know your software, they can imitate the systems you already trust.

If they know your public tone, they can write something that sounds like you.

That is how exposure connects to impersonation.

People say, "It is not hard for someone to clone you." They are right, and we need to connect the dots.

Cloning a person does not always mean creating a perfect digital twin. It can mean copying enough of your presence to fool someone who is not paying close attention. A name, a photo, a tone, a job title, a few mutual contacts, a familiar message style, and a believable reason for reaching out may be enough.

Cloning a business works the same way. A logo, a domain that looks close to the real one, a copied description, a fake social page, a payment link, and a few stolen images may be enough to fool a customer. A fake invoice with the right language may be enough to fool an employee. A message that appears to come from the owner may be enough to pressure a team member into action.

The clone does not have to be perfect.

It only has to be believable at the moment of decision.

That is why exposure is so powerful. It gives criminals the raw material to build believable lies.

Social media is one of the richest sources of that raw material.

A post that says, "I am traveling to speak at this event," may tell people you are away from home, busy, distracted, and possibly moving through airports or hotels. A post welcoming a new employee may tell criminals who to target before that employee knows company processes. A post thanking a vendor may reveal a business relationship that can be imitated later. A post about a big client meeting may tell outsiders what kind of business you are chasing. A post saying the office is closed this week may tell people when fewer eyes are watching.

A photo can reveal more than the caption. It can show badges, screens, documents, whiteboards, office layouts, tools, vehicles, addresses, or people who did not realize they were part of the post.

Again, the answer is not to stop sharing forever.

The answer is to share with strategy.

There is a difference between visibility and exposure. Visibility helps people know who you are, what you do, and why they should trust you. Exposure gives outsiders unnecessary details that can be used to manipulate, impersonate, or harm you.

A public speaker needs visibility. A business needs visibility. A brand needs visibility. A leader needs credibility. But none of that requires giving away every operational detail in real time.

You can post after an event instead of during it. You can thank a vendor without revealing internal systems. You can celebrate employees without exposing personal details. You can show success without showing dashboards, payment screens, client names, access portals, or private documents. You can be public without being reckless.

That is disciplined visibility.

The phone sits at the center of this problem.

Your phone is no longer just a phone. It is the master key to identity, money, communication, location, business access, and recovery. It holds email, text messages, banking apps, password resets, authentication codes, social media accounts, photos, cloud files, work chats, calendars, health apps, travel records, and sometimes access to company systems.

Take out your phone and look at your apps.

How many pages do you have? One? Three? Ten?

Every one of those apps is a door into some part of your life. Not because you did something wrong. Because modern technology works by exchanging convenience for access. We get the convenience immediately. We rarely understand the full price until something goes wrong.

Attackers know this. They are not only hunting people one at a time. They are hunting the companies on your phone. Your bank. Your email provider. Your payroll platform. Your insurance portal. Your phone carrier. Your cloud storage. Your accounting tool. Your customer systems. Your vendors. Your payment platforms.

They hunt scale.

If they can compromise a platform, steal credentials, hijack sessions, trick users, or imitate trusted workflows, they do not need to pick you out of a crowd. They wait for normal business to create the opening.

Normal logins.

Normal messages.

Normal approvals.

Normal password resets.

Normal vendor changes.

Normal links.

That is why the first breach is often informational before it is technical. The attacker learns enough to make the technical or financial move believable.

Convenience feeds this problem.

We save passwords in browsers. We stay logged in everywhere. We use one email for everything. We connect apps together because it is faster. We click social login buttons because it is easier. We give apps access to contacts, photos, microphones, cameras, and locations without thinking. We use personal phones for business. We keep old accounts active. We send files through open links. We use public Wi-Fi. We let work and personal life blend together until no one can tell where one risk ends and another begins.

Convenience is not evil.

Uncontrolled convenience is dangerous.

The same is true for public records and data brokers. Some exposure does not come from what you personally post. It comes from records, filings, registrations, property information, licensing databases, corporate documents, court records, and commercial data companies that collect and package information about people.

Your information can be collected, sold, combined, reused, and weaponized.

That is not theory. That is the modern data economy.

A person may believe they are private because they do not post much online, while their address, relatives, phone numbers, old emails, business registrations, and property records are sitting in searchable places. A business may believe it is careful while its filings, leadership structure, location, vendors, and employee profiles are giving outsiders enough to build a story.

This is why shame is not useful.

When people realize how exposed they are, they often react in one of three ways. They panic, they ignore it, or they buy the wrong tool. Panic makes people delete random things without understanding the risk. Ignoring it leaves the doors open. Buying the wrong tool creates false confidence.

The better response is to perform an exposure audit.

Not a complicated one at first. Start with questions.

What is public?

What is connected?

Who has access?

What can be copied?

What can be impersonated?

What can be used to reset an account?

What would hurt me if it became public?

What would hurt my business if it were stolen, altered, copied, or faked?

Those questions change the way you look at your life and business. They turn cybersecurity from a vague fear into a practical discipline.

After that, reduce unnecessary exposure.

Separate personal and business accounts where possible. Use better passwords and a password manager. Turn on strong multi-factor authentication. Review which apps have access to your contacts, photos, location, and microphone. Remove old accounts. Lock down social media. Stop posting sensitive operational details in real time. Train employees to verify before trusting. Use fewer tools where possible. Document who has access to what. Review vendors. Confirm payment changes through trusted channels. Prepare for recovery before damage happens.

None of this requires you to disappear.

It requires you to become intentional.

That is the authority people need in this conversation. Not fear. Not shame. Not technical noise. Authority means telling the truth clearly: the modern attacker does not need to start by breaking into your computer if you have already handed the internet enough information to make the attack work.

The world has changed. The battlefield has changed. The meaning of vulnerability has changed.

A vulnerability is no longer just a flaw in code.

A vulnerability can be a visible pattern, a public relationship, a personal detail, a business process, a connected app, a reused password, a helpful employee, a trusted vendor, an old account, or a phone full of doors no one has reviewed.

That is not meant to make you paranoid.

It is meant to make you awake.

The first step in protecting yourself is understanding what you are showing the world. The first step in protecting your business is understanding where your operations are visible, connected, copied, and trusted without verification.

In the modern world, the first breach is often not technical. It is informational. Long before someone breaks into an account, they may already know enough about you to make the attack work.

And once you understand that, exposure stops being invisible.

It becomes something you can reduce, manage, and control.

Chapter 6

The Lie of "I'm Too Small to Be Hacked"

You are not too small to be hacked.

You are small enough to be easier, faster, and cheaper to attack.

That is the truth many small business owners, families, contractors, creators, nonprofits, churches, local shops, and solo operators need to hear. It may not be comfortable, but comfort is not protection. The belief that no one would bother with you because you are not famous, not wealthy, not political, and not running a major corporation is one of the most dangerous beliefs in modern cybersecurity.

Criminals do not always care who you are. They care what door is unlocked.

That is where the phrase "I am too small to be hacked" becomes a problem. It creates a false sense of safety. When a business believes it is too small, it usually does not prepare. It delays security. It ignores weak passwords. It skips backups. It shares accounts. It lets employees use personal phones without rules. It leaves old users active. It assumes nothing valuable is at risk because the company is small.

That belief becomes the open door.

Small does not mean invisible. In many cases, small means easier to overlook, easier to automate against, easier to impersonate, and easier to underestimate. A small business may not have a security team. It may not have dedicated IT staff. It may not have a written incident plan. It may not have anyone reviewing access every month. It may not have a formal process for verifying vendor banking changes. It may not have clean onboarding and offboarding for employees. It may not have backups that have actually been tested.

None of that means the business is careless. It usually means the business is stretched thin.

Small business owners do everything. They sell, manage, hire, fire, pay bills, talk to customers, handle vendors, review payroll, answer emails, post on social media, fix problems, calm people down, and try to keep the doors open. Many small business owners are not ignoring security because they do not care. They are ignoring it because they are overwhelmed. They are trying to survive the day.

Cybercriminals do not care why the door is open. They only care that it is open.

This is why we have to stop thinking about cybercrime as if every attack begins with a criminal choosing one special victim. Some attacks are targeted, but many are industrial. They are built around volume. A criminal does not need one famous target if they can attack ten thousand small ones. They can test emails, passwords, fake invoices, websites, social media accounts, payment systems, and login portals at scale. They can scan. They can sort. They can test. They can move on when one target does not work and come back when another one does.

A business does not have to be famous to be found. It only has to be exposed.

Think about how a criminal looks at the world. They do not need your business to appear on the evening news. They need your email to answer. They need your payment process to be loose. They need your owner to be in a rush. They need your employee to believe the message is normal. They need your website to show enough information to imitate you. They need your customers to trust your name more than they question the link in front of them.

That is why small targets fit the criminal model so well. They are numerous. They are busy. They are often underprotected. They use many of the same platforms. They trust email because email is how business gets done. They trust invoices because invoices arrive every week. They trust payment links because customers expect speed. They trust social media pages because that is where modern marketing lives.

In other words, the criminal does not have to invent a new doorway. The business already uses the doorway every day. The attack hides inside normal operations.

That is what automation changed. Before automation, attacking people one by one took more time. Now a criminal or criminal network can send thousands of messages, test thousands of leaked passwords, scrape thousands of business listings, clone hundreds of pages, or probe many websites without personally knowing the owner of any of them. The victim may feel personally selected, but the attack may have started as a numbers game.

Artificial intelligence makes that numbers game more dangerous. AI can help criminals write cleaner emails, create fake customer messages, generate fake invoices, build fake job applications, produce fake reviews, draft fake legal threats, imitate business language, and create social media profiles that look more believable than the scams people were used to seeing years ago. The old warning signs are not enough anymore. Bad grammar used to be one of the clues people were taught to look for. Now a fake message can sound professional, polished, local, urgent, and personal.

That means small businesses cannot rely on being ignored. They also cannot rely on scams looking obvious.

A salon may think it has nothing a cybercriminal wants. But it may have client names, phone numbers, appointment history, payment records, employee information, gift card balances, and social media trust. A food truck may think it is too simple to be a target. But it uses payment apps, online ordering, location posts, vendor invoices, and bank accounts. A contractor may believe the work is physical, not digital. But that contractor may hold customer addresses, invoices, insurance documents, licenses, payment records, and messages about job sites.

A church may have donor information. A nonprofit may have volunteer lists, grant documents, banking access, and community trust. A daycare may have parent contacts, child records, emergency contacts, payment information, and schedules. A local shop may have vendor invoices, employee records, point-of-sale systems, customer messages, and social media pages. A real estate agent may handle wire-transfer communication, contracts, identification documents, lender contacts, and closing timelines. A creator or influencer may have brand deals, audience trust, payment accounts, private messages, and an online identity that can be copied.

None of those examples require a Fortune 500 company. They require connection, money, trust, and information. Small businesses have all four.

A small business may also carry something large companies spend years trying to build: local trust. Customers know the owner. Clients recognize the brand. Employees believe the message came from the boss. Vendors move quickly because the relationship is familiar. That trust is valuable, and criminals know it. They do not always need to create trust from nothing. They can borrow yours.

That is why a local business can be harmed by a fake page, a fake invoice, or a fake message faster than the owner expects. People who already trust the business may act quickly because they believe the relationship is real. The very thing that makes a small business strong in the community can be turned into a weapon if the business identity is not protected.

A small business is not just a small business. It is a bundle of money, access, trust, identity, and relationships.

That is what criminals want. They may want bank accounts. They may want client lists. They may want vendor relationships. They may want employee records. They may want payroll access. They may want tax documents. They may want invoices. They may want credit cards. They may want customer trust. They may want the business identity. They may want the social media page. They may want the company domain. They may want the email account.

Sometimes they do not even want to keep the business. They want to use it.

That is where small businesses become pathways to bigger targets. A small business may be connected to banks, payroll providers, insurance companies, vendors, customers, agencies, corporate partners, software platforms, payment processors, and other organizations. If criminals compromise a small business email account, invoice system, social page, or vendor relationship, they can use that trust to reach someone else. The small business becomes the doorway, the disguise, or the excuse.

A fake invoice sent from a compromised small business email may be trusted because the relationship already exists. A message from a real vendor account may pass through normal suspicion because people recognize the name. A cloned business page may collect money from customers who believe they are dealing with the real company. A fake job post may gather personal information from applicants who trust the brand. A fake partnership offer may use one company's identity to approach another.

This is how criminals turn small businesses into scapegoats.

They clone the business. They impersonate the owner. They copy the branding. They send fake invoices. They message customers. They redirect payments. They create fake social media pages. They build a look-alike website. They use the real company's name to give the fraud credibility. Then, when customers lose money or trust, the real business is left holding the blame.

The owner may not have committed the fraud, but the owner still has to explain it. The owner still has to answer angry messages. The owner still has to calm customers. The owner still has to file reports. The owner still has to work with banks, platforms, vendors, insurers, attorneys, or law enforcement. The owner still has to repair the reputation.

That is why identity protection matters for businesses, not only individuals.

A business has an identity. It has a name, a voice, a logo, a domain, a tone, a customer base, a reputation, and a pattern of communication. When that identity is copied or abused, the damage is not only technical. It is emotional. It is financial. It is operational. It is reputational.

And for a small business, that kind of damage can become a survival issue quickly.

One incident can trigger a chain reaction. It can begin as a banking problem, then become a payroll problem, then become a legal problem, then become a customer trust problem, then become a vendor dispute, then become a reputation problem, then become an insurance problem, then become an operational shutdown. By the time the owner realizes how far the damage has spread, the original cyber issue may feel like the smallest part of the crisis.

This is the reality that too many people underestimate. A cyberattack does not stay in the cyber lane. It crosses lanes. It moves into finance. It moves into operations. It moves into customer service. It moves into legal exposure. It moves into sales. It moves into employee morale. It moves into leadership credibility. It moves into sleep, health, family stress, and emotional exhaustion.

For a large company, a cyber incident may be serious but survivable because there are departments, reserves, attorneys, insurance teams, public relations people, and technical responders. For a small business, the same type of incident may land on one owner who is already carrying everything.

That is why recovery is often misunderstood.

Many small businesses think recovery means getting the account back, filing the police report, changing the password, calling the bank, or restoring a file. Those steps matter, but they are only part of recovery. Real recovery is not just restoring systems. It is restoring confidence.

Time may not come back. Customer trust may not come back. Missed opportunities may not come back. Momentum may not come back. The owner may spend weeks or months proving what happened, rebuilding access, calming customers, resetting accounts, contacting vendors, explaining the situation, watching for more fraud, and trying to run the business while exhausted.

That is not a minor inconvenience. That is a second job forced onto someone who already had a full one.

This is also where cost becomes misunderstood. People ask, "How much does cybersecurity cost?" That is a fair question. But the better question is, "How much does disorder cost after something goes wrong?" How much does it cost to lose a week of operations? How much does it cost to miss payroll? How much does it cost when customers hesitate to pay invoices because they are not sure which message is real? How much does it cost when the owner cannot focus on sales because every hour is spent proving identity to banks and platforms?

The cheapest security is usually the security you build before the incident. Not because every tool is cheap, but because discipline is cheaper than chaos. A verified payment process is cheaper than a stolen transfer. Removing an old employee account is cheaper than cleaning up misuse. A password manager is cheaper than account takeover. A backup is cheaper than starting over. Training an employee to pause is cheaper than rebuilding trust after one rushed click.

I understand that damage as a founder. A scam, breach, impersonation, account issue, or trust attack does not only cost money. It steals time, focus, momentum, and confidence. When you are building from the ground up, losing momentum can feel like losing years. People on the outside may only see the transaction or the account. The owner feels the weight of what could have been built during the time spent cleaning up the damage.

That is why the conversation has to change from panic to preparation.

You do not need to panic. You need to prepare.

Preparation does not have to begin with expensive enterprise tools. Security begins with discipline before it becomes software. A small business can start by knowing every tool it uses. Who has access? Which accounts matter most? Which systems hold money? Which systems hold customer information? Which systems control payroll? Which systems can reset other systems? Which employees have admin permissions? Which vendors can touch operations? Which old accounts are still active?

Those questions are not technical trivia. They are leadership questions.

The owner is the first security officer.

That title does not require the owner to become a technician. It requires the owner to set priorities. What must never be exposed? Who is allowed to move money? Who can approve access? Who can change payroll? Who can speak for the company online? Who owns the domain? Who controls the social media pages? Who can reset accounts? Who knows what to do if the business email is compromised?

Those questions do not belong only to IT. They belong to leadership because they define how the business survives. If no one can answer them before an incident, everyone will be guessing during one.

Not because the owner is technical. Not because the owner should become the IT department. The owner is the first security officer because the owner controls the money, the payroll, the tools, the vendors, the hiring, the customer trust, and the reputation of the business. If the owner treats security like an afterthought, the team will too. If the owner treats security like survival, the business becomes harder to exploit.

Leadership sets the standard. If payment changes can happen through one email, that is a leadership decision. If employees share passwords, that is a leadership decision. If former employees keep access, that is a leadership decision. If no one verifies vendors, that is a leadership decision. If backups are ignored, that is a leadership decision. If personal phones are used for business without rules, that is a leadership decision.

This is not about blame. It is about ownership.

Once a business owner accepts that the business is not too small, the first step is visibility and control. Know every tool the business uses. Review who has access.

Separate business and personal accounts where possible. Use unique passwords. Turn on multi-factor authentication. Verify vendor payment changes through trusted channels. Back up important data. Train employees. Remove old users immediately. Create a simple incident plan. Monitor the business identity online.

The goal is not perfection on day one. The goal is closing the easiest doors first.

Start with a simple standard. No shared passwords for critical accounts. No payment change without independent verification. No former employee left active. No business social media account controlled by only one person's personal login. No important data without a backup. No payroll or banking access without stronger authentication. No assumption that a message is real because it looks professional.

These are not luxury controls. These are basic controls. They are the digital equivalent of locking the front door, checking the cash drawer, knowing who has keys, and keeping copies of important records. No one calls those habits extreme in the physical world. We should not treat them as extreme in the digital world either.

Start with the doors criminals love: weak passwords, shared accounts, unverified payment changes, old users, exposed social media pages, personal devices with business access, and no backup plan. Those are not advanced nation-state problems. Those are everyday business problems. Fixing them does not make the business invincible, but it makes the business less easy.

That matters because criminals often choose the path of least resistance. If your business is harder than the next exposed business, you have improved your odds. That may not sound glamorous, but cybersecurity is not about glamour. It is about reducing risk in practical ways before damage becomes expensive.

For small businesses, one of the most important habits is verification. Verify before money moves. Verify before banking details change. Verify before payroll information is updated. Verify before admin access is granted. Verify before clicking a link connected to payment, identity, credentials, or sensitive records.

Verify through a known, trusted channel, not the contact information inside the suspicious message.

Another important habit is separation. Separate personal and business accounts where possible. Separate employee access by role. Separate owner access from everyday browsing. Separate administrative privileges from normal use. Separate public visibility from private operations. Separation limits how far damage can spread when something goes wrong.

Another habit is removal. Remove what you do not need. Remove old users. Remove abandoned tools. Remove stale accounts. Remove unnecessary app permissions. Remove public details that create risk without creating value. Remove the belief that more tools automatically means more protection.

A small business does not become safer by collecting dashboards. It becomes safer by knowing what matters, reducing confusion, and controlling the moments where criminals cause the most damage.

That is the theme running through Part I of this book. The world changed, and most people missed it. Everything became connected. Cybersecurity stopped being only an IT problem. Everyone became a target because attackers chase exposure, scale, and opportunity. The battlefield moved into phones, inboxes, apps, businesses, banks, and trust relationships. Exposure became the new vulnerability. And now we have to confront the final lie that keeps people unprotected: the belief that smallness is safety.

It is not.

Small does not mean invisible. Small does not mean unimportant. Small does not mean safe. Small does not mean criminals will politely pass you by. Small often means the business has valuable information, trusted relationships, real money moving through real accounts, and fewer defenses protecting it.

Security is not only for big companies. It is part of running a responsible business in the modern world. It is part of protecting clients, employees, vendors, families, donors, customers, and communities. It is part of protecting the trust that keeps a business alive.

If you are a solo operator, you are not too small. If you have one employee, you are not too small. If you have one client, you are not too small. If you accept payments, you are not too small. If you store customer information, you are not too small. If your name is attached to your work, you are not too small. If people trust you, you are not too small.

You are connected.

And connected means reachable.

That does not mean you should live afraid. It means you should live prepared. It means you should stop measuring risk by the size of your company and start measuring risk by the value of what you protect. Money. Identity. Trust. Time. Relationships. Reputation. Operations. People.

Those things are worth protecting, no matter how small the business appears from the outside.

This is the lesson that closes Part I. Cybersecurity is not a distant technical issue anymore. It is the discipline of protecting life and business in a connected world. Once everything is connected, size stops being the measure of risk. Exposure becomes the measure of risk. Access becomes the measure of risk. Trust becomes the measure of risk.

A small business is not small to the people who depend on it. It may be a family's income, an employee's paycheck, a customer's trusted service, a donor's chosen cause, a client's confidential record, or a founder's years of sacrifice. To the outside world, it may look small. To the people connected to it, it is not small at all.

You are not too small to be hacked. You are too connected, too trusted, and too valuable to stay unprotected.

Small does not mean invisible; it means you have to protect the trust, money, people, and reputation that keep your business alive.

Part II:

The Attacks Hiding in Plain Sight

Chapter 7

The Business Model of Cybercrime

Cybercrime is not small anymore.

In 2022, estimates already placed global cybercrime damage in the trillions. By 2025, widely cited industry forecasts from Cybersecurity Ventures estimate cybercrime will cost the world about $10.5 trillion annually.

That number matters because it changes how we talk about the threat.

This is not a side hustle. This is not one person guessing passwords. This is not a few bad emails floating around the internet.

This is an economy.

If cybercrime were measured like a country, it would be one of the largest economies in the world. That means criminals are not just stealing randomly. They are building systems, testing what works, selling access, reusing stolen data, impersonating trusted names, and moving money faster than most victims can react.

And the scariest part is this: most victims do not see the business model.

They only see the message, the invoice, the fake website, the phone call, the investment pitch, the password reset, the job offer, or the person pretending to be someone they trust. They see the thing placed directly in front of them. They do not see the machinery behind it.

That machinery is what we need to understand.

Cybercrime works because criminals treat it like a business while too many victims still treat it like bad luck. Criminals look for leads. They test targets. They buy tools. They sell access. They reuse stolen information. They build fake legitimacy. They impersonate trusted people and organizations. They scale what works and abandon what does not.

Cybercrime is a business model because stolen trust, stolen identity, stolen access, and stolen data can all be turned into money.

That is the shift. We are not only dealing with someone trying to break into a computer. We are dealing with an organized market built around converting human trust into profit.

Most people still carry an outdated picture of the cybercriminal. They imagine one lonely hacker in a dark room, wearing a hoodie, guessing passwords and breaking into machines for the thrill of it. That person may exist, but that image is too small for the threat we face today.

The modern threat can include organized scam groups, stolen-data sellers, identity brokers, access sellers, phishing operators, fake website builders, romance scammers, ransomware groups, money mules, and AI-assisted impersonators. Some are technical. Some are not. Some never touch malware. Some never write code. Some never speak to a victim directly. They do one job inside a larger system.

That is what makes this economy dangerous. The crime can be divided into roles.

The person who tricks you may not be the person who stole your password. The person who stole your password may not be the person who drains the account. The person who drains the account may not be the person who built the fake website. The person who built the fake website may not be the person who moves the money. By the time a victim realizes what happened, the crime may have already passed through several hands.

Victims often look for the scammer, singular. But the modern scam may be a supply chain.

One person steals credentials. Another sells access. Another writes phishing messages. Another builds fake websites. Another impersonates a business. Another launders money. Another runs social media scams. Another buys stolen accounts. Another turns stolen information into fake loans, fake refunds, fake payroll changes, or fake invoices.

This specialization makes cybercrime faster, cheaper, and harder to stop. It also makes the victim's experience more confusing. The person on the phone may sound confident because their only job is to sound confident. The email may be polished because someone else wrote it. The website may look real because another person built it. The payment route may be difficult to trace because someone else handles movement of money.

That is how a criminal operation begins to look less like chaos and more like a company, except the product is theft.

In that economy, stolen information becomes inventory.

Passwords are inventory. Identities are inventory. Bank access is inventory. Business email access is inventory. Credit card data is inventory. Customer lists are inventory. Tax records are inventory. Medical information is inventory. Social media accounts are inventory. Payroll access is inventory. Company system access is inventory. Vendor contacts are inventory. Domains, invoices, contracts, and account histories can all become inventory.

To the victim, it is personal. It is a life, a business, a reputation, a customer relationship, a bank account, or a private record. To the criminal economy, it is product.

That distinction is important because criminals do not always use what they steal immediately. They may sell it. They may combine it. They may wait. They may test it against other systems. They may use one piece of information to make the next piece easier to steal.

Access itself is one of the most valuable products in this economy.

A criminal does not always need to steal the money personally. Sometimes they steal access and sell it to someone else. Access to an email account. Access to a bank login. Access to a payroll system. Access to a company dashboard. Access to a social media page. Access to a vendor portal. Access to a person's identity. Access is valuable because it lets someone else commit the next crime.

That is why one compromised account can matter even if nothing obvious happens right away. If someone gets into your email, they may not empty anything on day one. They may read. They may learn. They may search for invoices, contracts, vendors, password resets, bank alerts, employee names, customer disputes, and personal details. They may wait until the right moment to send the right message from the right place.

Silence does not always mean safety. Sometimes silence means the attacker is still learning.

Stolen data also does not expire just because you changed one password. A breach can echo for months or years. An old email address can be used in password testing. An old password can be tried across other sites. A leaked invoice can be used to imitate a vendor. A stolen employee list can be used for phishing. A customer list can be used for targeted scams. A tax document can be used for identity theft. Medical information can be used for fraud. A business domain can be used to build believable fake pages.

A stolen email address may seem small. A stolen password may seem fixable. A stolen invoice may seem boring. But criminals combine small pieces into a bigger picture.

This is why cybercrime has a supply chain.

There are data thieves. Credential sellers. Scam writers. Fake website builders. Money mules. Impersonators. Technical hackers. AI tool users. Ransomware groups. Laundering networks. Some parts of that chain collect information. Some parts package it. Some parts sell it. Some parts use it. Some parts hide the money. Some parts repeat the process with the next victim.

A business owner may only see the fake invoice, but that fake invoice may be the final step in a long chain. Someone found the business. Someone gathered the vendor information. Someone created or compromised an email account. Someone wrote the message. Someone prepared the receiving account. Someone moved the money.

That is why the scam can feel so professional. It has been prepared.

Automation is what makes that preparation profitable at scale. A criminal does not need every attack to work. If an operation sends 100,000 messages and only a small percentage respond, the operation can still make money. They can test passwords at scale. Scan websites at scale. Send fake invoices at scale. Scrape social media at scale. Clone business pages at scale. Attackers do not need to know every victim personally because the system can find the exposed ones.

This is the answer to the person who says, "Why would they target me?" They may not have targeted you personally. The system found you. Your email was on a list. Your password was reused. Your business page was public. Your invoice process was visible. Your vendor relationship was exposed. Your phone number was available. Your domain looked useful. Your role had authority.

Cybercrime becomes profitable when the attacker can process people faster than people can verify what is happening.

Artificial intelligence improves that model. AI does not create the criminal instinct, but it can strengthen the criminal workflow. It can help create better scam emails, better fake voices, better fake profiles, better fake businesses, better fake invoices, better fake customer support, better research on victims, faster message creation, more convincing impersonation, fake reviews, fake job postings, and fake legal threats.

AI lowers the effort required to look professional. That is a major change. People used to rely on obvious mistakes as warning signs. Bad grammar. Strange wording. Sloppy logos. Ugly websites. Awkward messages. Those clues can still appear, but they are no longer enough. A scam can now sound polished. It can sound educated. It can sound local. It can sound like your industry. It can sound like the kind of message you receive every day.

Professional-looking no longer means legitimate.

A polished website does not prove trust. A logo does not prove authority. A nice invoice does not prove the payment is real. A clean email does not prove the sender is safe. A fake review does not prove a business exists. A document with legal language does not prove a contract is valid. A confident person on the phone does not prove they are who they claim to be.

Modern scams are not always sloppy. Some are designed to pass the first glance.

That first glance is where busy people get caught. The message looks close enough. The name is familiar enough. The request is normal enough. The urgency is believable enough. The logo is professional enough. The website is polished enough. The victim acts before they verify.

That is the trap. The scam does not need to look evil. It only needs to look normal long enough for you to act.

Social media feeds the business model by giving criminals research, disguise, and delivery. It tells them who you trust, where you work, who your family is, what you buy, what business you run, what events you attend, what causes you support, who your customers are, who your vendors are, and how you communicate in public.

It also gives them a stage. Fake profiles. Trust-building. Impersonation. Romance scams. Job scams. Investment scams. Customer scams. Fake giveaways. Business cloning. Reputation attacks. Social media turns public information into criminal preparation.

A criminal may study a leader's posts before impersonating that leader. They may study a business page before creating a fake version of it. They may watch customer comments before sending fake support messages. They may look at event announcements before targeting a speaker, attendee, sponsor, or vendor. They may use public photos to make a fake profile feel familiar.

Again, the information may not look dangerous by itself. But in the criminal economy, small details become tools.

Fake businesses fit into this model because they provide camouflage. Criminals create fake companies, fake websites, fake support pages, fake investment groups, fake stores, fake charities, fake agencies, fake recruiters, and fake vendor portals. The goal is not always to look perfect. The goal is to look real enough long enough.

A real-looking logo. A domain that looks close enough. A realistic invoice. A professional email. Fake reviews. Fake customer service. Fake urgency. That can be enough to move money, collect data, or steal trust.

This is where my own experience as a founder still matters, but from a different angle than the personal damage. When I went through the angel investor scam I described earlier, the lesson was not only that one person lied. The lesson was that the scam had structure. It had fake legitimacy. It had paperwork. It had verification theater. It had confidence. It had pressure. It had money movement. It was designed to make doubt feel unreasonable.

That phrase matters: verification theater.

Verification theater is when a scam gives you enough paperwork, websites, names, steps, or explanations to make you feel like verification has happened, even though the thing that actually matters has not been independently confirmed. The scam builds a stage, hands you a script, and pressures you to act before you step outside the scene and verify it through a separate channel.

That is how modern scams operate. They do not always ask you to believe nothing. They ask you to believe the wrong proof.

They borrow the appearance of legitimacy from the systems we already trust. Banks. Vendors. Employers. Government agencies. Churches. Nonprofits. Influencers. Local businesses. Attorneys. Recruiters. Platforms. The criminal does not need you to trust them as a stranger. They need you to trust the name they are pretending to be.

Trust is what they steal before they steal the money.

That is why normal business processes are such effective camouflage. Invoices. Payroll updates. Vendor changes. Customer support. Job applications. Contracts. Shipping updates. Subscription notices. Password resets. Bank alerts. Legal notices. Refund requests. Donation requests. Account verification messages. These do not feel strange because they are part of ordinary life and ordinary work.

A fake invoice does not look like a cyberattack. It looks like accounting. A fake payroll update does not look like a cyberattack. It looks like HR. A fake password reset does not look like a cyberattack. It looks like support. A fake legal notice does not look like a cyberattack. It looks like pressure. A fake job application does not look like a cyberattack. It looks like hiring.

That is why cybercrime works so well against busy people. It hides inside the routines people already follow.

For criminals, this can be a high-reward, low-friction business. Victims may live in different states or countries. Evidence may be hard to collect. Accounts may disappear. Money may move quickly. Platforms may respond slowly. Reporting may feel confusing. Recovery may be difficult. The criminal's risk can feel low compared to the potential reward.

That does not mean reporting is useless. It means prevention matters because recovery is not guaranteed.

Report it. Document it. Preserve evidence. Save emails, headers, screenshots, phone numbers, account names, payment details, domain names, messages, and timelines. But do not build your entire safety plan around being rescued after the damage is done. Law enforcement matters. Reports matter. Evidence matters. But many victims never recover the full money, time, trust, reputation, or momentum they lost.

Prevention is not paranoia. It is cheaper than recovery.

So what should a reader do when something looks legitimate? Pause long enough to test the business model behind the request.

Ask: Who benefits from me acting quickly? Can I verify this through another channel? Is this request normal for this relationship? Did the payment instructions change? Is the urgency real or manufactured? Is this website or domain exactly correct? Who controls the account I am interacting with? Have I contacted the person through a trusted number or known channel? Am I being pushed to secrecy? Am I being told not to talk to anyone else? Is this asking for money, access, identity, or trust?

Those questions are not delays. They are defense.

The pause is protection.

For leaders and business owners, this is where the lesson becomes practical. Do not only ask whether a message looks real. Ask what business process the message is trying to move. Is it trying to move money? Change access? Capture identity? Pressure payroll? Redirect a vendor? Influence a customer? Damage reputation? Once you identify the process being touched, the message stops being just a message. It becomes a risk event.

That language matters. A vendor banking change is not just an email. It is a money-movement event. A password reset is not just a support task. It is an access event. A request for employee information is not just paperwork. It is an identity event. A fake customer complaint is not just a service problem. It can become a reputation event. A job application with attachments is not just recruiting. It can become a system-entry event.

Cybercrime succeeds when organizations treat high-risk moments like ordinary routine. The criminal wants the invoice to feel like every other invoice. They want the payroll update to feel like every other payroll update. They want the legal notice to feel like every other frightening document. They want the fake customer message to feel like something your team should handle quickly and quietly. Their business model depends on you not pausing long enough to classify the risk.

A stronger organization does the opposite. It labels the moment. It slows down the decision. It moves verification outside the message. It preserves evidence before deleting anything. It asks who owns the account, who authorized the change, and whether the request matches the normal relationship. It does not punish people for asking questions. It builds questions into the workflow.

This is not about making business slow. It is about making fraud less efficient. Criminals love speed because speed reduces judgment. They love urgency because urgency makes people skip steps. They love secrecy because secrecy isolates the victim from people who might stop the mistake. They love authority because authority makes employees comply. They love confusion because confusion makes people guess.

A good defense adds friction in exactly the right places. Not everywhere. Not so much friction that work becomes impossible. But enough friction around the moments that can cost money, identity, trust, or access. Money movement deserves friction. Administrative access deserves friction. Payroll changes deserve friction. Vendor changes deserve friction. Public statements during a crisis deserve friction. Anything that can create irreversible damage deserves verification.

That is how you fight a business model with a better business process.

The same applies personally. If a message asks for money, identity, access, secrecy, or speed, it deserves a pause. If a person claims to be someone you trust but contacts you through a new channel, it deserves a pause. If a website looks professional but the domain is unfamiliar, it deserves a pause. If the request makes you feel embarrassed to ask someone else, it deserves a pause. If the person on the other end tells you not to talk to anyone, it deserves more than a pause. It deserves suspicion.

None of this requires paranoia. It requires a decision that trust is valuable and should not be handed over simply because something looks familiar. The criminal economy is built on borrowed trust. The defensive economy must be built on verified trust.

That is the leadership lesson of this chapter. If cybercrime is an economy, then every person and business needs a system that makes them harder to process. Not impossible to attack. Harder to process. Harder to impersonate. Harder to rush. Harder to confuse. Harder to use as a doorway to someone else.

Cybercrime is not random anymore. It is organized. It is profitable. It is scalable. It has tools. It has roles. It has sellers and buyers. It has people who steal passwords, people who sell access, people who build fake websites, people who write the messages, people who impersonate businesses, and people who move the money.

That should scare people more than the old image of one hacker in a basement, because this is not one person guessing your password. This is a system built to process human trust.

But understanding the system also gives you power. Once you know cybercrime is organized, you can stop treating every message as a one-time mystery. You can look for the pattern. What process is being abused? What trust is being borrowed? What access is being requested? What urgency is being manufactured? What verification path exists outside the message? What evidence needs to be preserved before anything is deleted?

That is the difference between panic and control.

The goal is not to live afraid. The goal is to stop being easy to process. You do that by slowing down the moment criminals want you to speed up. You do it by verifying through channels they do not control. You do it by treating access as valuable. You do it by protecting identity and trust as seriously as you protect money. You do it by remembering that fake legitimacy is part of the attack, not proof that the attack is harmless.

Cybercrime is not random; it is a business built to turn trust into money.

And the modern criminal does not always break down the door; sometimes they walk in wearing the name of someone you already trust.

Chapter 8

Phishing, Scams, and the Art of Looking Legitimate

Phishing does not look like it used to.

That is the first thing people need to understand. Too many still imagine phishing as a badly written email filled with strange spelling, awkward grammar, obvious lies, and a message from someone claiming to be a foreign prince. That kind of scam still exists, but it is not the standard people should build their safety around.

Modern phishing can be polished. It can be polite. It can be branded. It can be timed around something real happening in your life or business. It can use your name. It can use a real logo. It can reference a real transaction. It can copy the tone of a real company. It can come from a compromised account. It can use artificial intelligence to sound normal.

The mistake people make is assuming they will recognize the scam by how it looks.

They may not.

Phishing is not just email anymore, and it is not just a suspicious link in a message. Phishing is someone pretending to be trusted so they can trick you into giving them something valuable. That something may be money, passwords, business access, bank access, identity information, client records, payroll information, vendor payment details, social media control, documents, or trust.

Phishing is not about the message itself. The message is only the delivery system. Phishing is about the trap.

That trap may arrive by email. It may arrive by text message. It may arrive through a phone call, a social media direct message, a QR code, a fake website, an online ad, a voice message, a job platform, a payment app, a messaging app, a fake support chat, a document-signing platform, or a business portal. The old advice, "Do not open suspicious emails," is no longer enough. The better advice is this: do not trust a request simply because it arrived through a familiar channel.

Familiar does not mean safe.

That is difficult for people because modern life depends on messages. We receive bank alerts, package updates, subscription renewals, invoices, payroll notices, password resets, customer complaints, delivery problems, tax notices, government notices, legal threats, job offers, investment opportunities, charity requests, account verification messages, document-signing requests, refund notices, and insurance requests. Most of these messages are ordinary. Some are real. Some are important. Some require action.

That is why phishing works.

It hides inside normal communication.

The most dangerous scam is not always the one that looks strange. It is the one that looks ordinary enough to get through your routine. It looks like something you see every week. It uses the kind of language you expect. It asks for the kind of action you already take. It lands while you are busy, distracted, tired, traveling, managing payroll, handling a customer, or trying to get through the day.

The scam does not need to look evil.

It only needs to look normal long enough for you to act.

A professional-looking scam is still a scam.

That line matters enough to repeat: a professional-looking scam is still a scam.

A logo does not prove authority. A polished website does not prove trust. A clean invoice does not prove the payment is real. A professional email does not prove the sender is safe. A familiar name does not prove the account is controlled by the person you know. A phone number inside the message does not prove the message is legitimate. A document with legal language does not prove the threat is real. A social media profile with photos does not prove the person exists. A caller who sounds calm and prepared does not prove they are telling the truth.

Appearance is no longer enough.

Scammers have better tools now. They can copy logos. They can clone websites. They can scrape public information. They can use artificial intelligence to write clean messages. They can create fake reviews. They can imitate communication styles. They can research victims. They can build fake business pages that look real enough to pass a quick glance. They can create fake customer service chats, fake legal notices, fake invoices, fake job postings, and fake support pages.

The obvious warning signs are disappearing.

Years ago, bad grammar, strange formatting, and awkward wording were easier to spot. Today, a phishing message can sound educated. It can sound corporate. It can sound local. It can sound like your industry. It can sound like someone who knows exactly what they are doing.

That is not because every criminal became brilliant. It is because the tools got better.

Artificial intelligence makes phishing faster, cleaner, and more personal. It can help criminals create better grammar, better personalization, better fake voices, better cloned writing styles, better fake documents, more targeted scams, more realistic fake businesses, fake customer service chats, fake legal threats, fake job applications, fake reviews, and fake social media profiles. It lowers the effort required to look legitimate.

That means verification matters more than instinct.

Instinct still has value. If something feels wrong, slow down. But instinct alone is not a security strategy. People are busy. People are helpful. People are tired. People trust familiar names. People want to do their jobs well. A message can feel normal and still be dangerous.

Scammers understand that. They do not only exploit ignorance. They exploit good traits.

A bookkeeper pays quickly because they want the vendor taken care of. An assistant responds quickly because they do not want to disappoint the owner. An employee clicks the HR link because they want their payroll fixed. A parent responds to a school message because they are worried. A founder answers an investor message because they need opportunity. A customer service person opens an attachment because they want to solve the customer's problem.

Many people do not get scammed because they are foolish. They get scammed because they are trying to be helpful, polite, fast, professional, responsive, or responsible.

That is why shame is dangerous.

Shame keeps people quiet. Quiet helps criminals. If an employee is afraid of being embarrassed, they may not report the message. If a parent feels foolish, they may not ask for help. If a business owner feels responsible for missing the signs, they may delay telling customers, banks, vendors, or staff. The longer the silence lasts, the more time the attacker has.

A healthy security culture does not shame people for receiving a scam. It trains them to pause, report, and verify before damage spreads.

The strongest phishing messages usually use one or more emotional triggers: urgency, fear, helpfulness, authority, secrecy, or opportunity.

Urgency is one of the most powerful. The message says, "Act now." "Your account will be closed." "Payment is overdue." "Final notice." "Confirm immediately." "Your package is delayed." "Your payroll failed." "Your bank account is locked." "Your access will expire." "Legal action pending."

The goal is to make you act before you verify.

Urgency shortens the space between fear and action. That space is where safety lives.

Fear makes people move fast. Scammers use fear of losing money, missing a delivery, being sued, losing access, disappointing a boss, missing payroll, losing a job opportunity, or looking irresponsible. They know people do not want to be the reason something fails. So the scam says: fix this now. Confirm this now. Pay this now. Click this now. Send this now.

Fear turns a normal person into a rushed person.

Rushed people skip verification.

Authority works the same way. A message that appears to come from the owner, a bank, a government agency, an attorney, a platform, a payroll provider, or a major vendor gets treated differently than a message from a stranger. People have been trained to respond to authority. In business, that habit can be useful. In phishing, it becomes dangerous when authority is borrowed by the wrong person.

The criminal does not need you to trust them. They need you to trust the name they are wearing.

That is why phishing is a trust attack.

It is not only a technical attack. It is not only a message attack. In business, phishing is often a process attack. The attacker is trying to move something inside your operation. Money. Access. Identity. Payroll. Vendor details. Customer information. Reputation. A password reset. A document approval. An account change.

If we treat phishing only as a suspicious email problem, we miss the business process being abused.

Consider a common example. A bookkeeper receives an email that looks like it came from a known vendor. The message says the vendor changed banks and needs future payments sent to a new account. The logo is correct. The signature looks familiar. The invoice format looks normal. The message is polite. The amount matches what the business usually pays.

So the bookkeeper updates the payment details.

But the vendor was never the sender. The attacker may have spoofed the email, compromised an old conversation, copied the vendor's identity, or studied the relationship before sending the request. The business pays the criminal. The real vendor still expects payment. Now the owner has a banking problem, a vendor problem, a trust problem, and possibly an insurance problem.

That is phishing as a business attack.

No dramatic hacking scene. No pop-up warning. No strange code on the screen. Just a believable message at the speed of business.

This is why fake vendor banking changes are so dangerous. The email is not the real issue. The issue is money movement. If a request changes where money goes, it should never be treated as just another email thread. It should be treated as a high-risk event requiring independent verification.

The same is true for payroll changes. A message saying an employee changed bank accounts may look like routine HR work. But if that message is fake, the next paycheck may go to a criminal. A document-signing request may look like normal business. But if the link leads to a fake login page, it can steal credentials. A fake customer complaint may look like a service issue. But if it includes an attachment, link, or demand for private information, it may be the opening move in a larger attack.

Business phishing often aims at money, access, or authority. The biggest risks include fake vendor banking changes, fake CEO or owner requests, fake invoices, fake payroll changes, fake customer complaints, fake login pages, fake document-signing requests, fake HR messages, fake job applications with attachments, fake legal notices, fake tax forms, fake insurance requests, fake refund requests, fake subscription renewals, fake support tickets, and fake cloud storage links.

None of these have to feel strange when they arrive.

That is the danger.

The more ordinary the message feels, the less likely the person is to slow down.

Phishing also connects directly to identity theft. Many scams begin by collecting small pieces of identity. A message may ask for a name, email, phone number, address, date of birth, last four digits, login code, password, security answers, photo ID, bank information, social media access, payroll information, or tax forms. The first request may seem small. But once criminals collect enough, they can take over accounts, open fake accounts, impersonate the victim, redirect money, or trick someone else using the victim's identity.

Phishing is often the front door to identity theft.

It also connects to business email compromise, one of the most dangerous forms of phishing. Once criminals get inside an email account, they can read old conversations, study relationships, learn invoice patterns, copy writing style, watch for upcoming payments, and send messages from inside the real account.

That changes everything.

The message may not come from a fake address. It may come from the real account. The language may sound familiar because the attacker has read the previous conversation. The timing may be perfect because the attacker has been watching. The request may feel legitimate because it is inserted into an existing relationship.

At that point, the warning signs are harder to see.

That is why businesses cannot rely only on whether an email looks right. They need rules for high-risk actions. If payment instructions change, verify outside the message. If payroll details change, verify outside the message. If an employee asks for unusual access, verify outside the message. If a legal threat demands urgent action, verify outside the message. If a customer asks for sensitive data, verify outside the message. If a request involves money, identity, passwords, business access, payroll, legal pressure, or urgency, do not click from the message.

Go directly through the official app, official website, saved bookmark, or known phone number.

That rule may sound simple, but simple rules are often the ones people remember under pressure.

When money, identity, passwords, business access, payroll, legal threats, or urgency are involved, do not click from the message.

Verify outside the message.

Verification is not distrust.

Verification is how trust survives.

A business owner should train employees to understand that reporting a suspicious message is not "bothering the boss." Reporting is protection. Employees should be trained to pause before payments, verify vendor banking changes, never share passwords, never approve urgent money requests through email alone, never trust a link just because it has a logo, use known channels, escalate anything involving money, identity, access, payroll, legal threats, vendor changes, or customer data, and preserve evidence before deleting.

The employee should not feel punished for asking a security question. The employee should feel expected to ask.

A company that punishes people for slowing down high-risk decisions is training them to help the attacker.

This is also why evidence matters. When a suspicious message arrives, the first reaction should not always be to delete it immediately. If the message involves money, identity, business access, legal threats, payroll, customers, or a possible incident, preserve what happened. Screenshot the message. Save the email. Keep the sender information. Preserve the URL. Record the timestamp. Do not click. Do not reply. Do not download attachments. Verify through another channel. Report it internally if at work. Block or delete only after the evidence is preserved if needed.

This matters because recovery depends on proof. Banks, platforms, insurers, law enforcement, vendors, and internal teams may all need to know what happened. If the evidence disappears, the response becomes harder. The strongest security programs do not only warn the user. They explain the risk in plain English, recommend the next action, preserve evidence, create an incident timeline, and help the user verify before acting.

That is the direction cybersecurity has to move. It cannot only scan files and say whether an attachment is clean. It has to understand the moment. Is this asking for money? Is this asking for identity? Is this asking for passwords or codes? Is this asking for business access? Is it changing payment instructions? Is it creating urgency? Is it using fear? Is it borrowing authority? Is it asking for secrecy? Is it coming through a new or unusual channel? Is the domain slightly wrong? Is the sender asking for action outside the normal process?

Those questions classify the risk by what the message is trying to trigger, not only by how the message looks.

That is how phishing should be understood in the modern world. Not as a bad email problem. As an attempt to trigger action before verification.

This applies to individuals and families too. A parent receives a message about a child's school account. A person gets a text saying a package is delayed. Someone receives a bank alert asking them to confirm activity. A social media message says a friend needs help. A romance scam builds emotional trust before asking for money. An investment message offers opportunity with urgency. A fake charity request uses compassion. A fake support page asks for login details.

The details change. The structure does not.

Someone pretends to be trusted. They create pressure. They ask for action. They try to move you before you verify.

The answer is not to stop trusting everyone. A life without trust is not workable, and a business without trust cannot operate. The answer is to stop confusing appearance with proof.

Trust should have a process.

For individuals, that process may be as simple as going directly to the official app instead of clicking a link. Calling a known number. Asking a family member through another channel. Checking the real website by typing it manually. Refusing to share codes. Saving evidence when something feels serious.

For businesses, that process must be written, trained, and repeated. Vendor payment changes require verification. Payroll changes require verification. Admin access requires verification. Legal notices require verification. Customer data requests require verification. Anything that can move money, identity, access, or reputation should not be approved by appearance alone.

This is the discipline phishing tries to break.

It wants speed. You create pause.

It wants secrecy. You create reporting.

It wants fear. You create process.

It wants appearance to be enough. You require proof.

It wants one person isolated in a moment of pressure. You build a culture where people escalate before they act.

That is how the target becomes harder.

Phishing does not look like it used to. It can look like your bank. It can look like your payroll system. It can look like a vendor you already know. It can look like a delivery update, a legal notice, a job offer, a customer complaint, or a message from your boss. With AI, it can sound polished. It can sound calm. It can sound professional. It can sound like someone who knows exactly what they are doing.

That is the trap.

A scam does not need to look fake to be fake.

It only needs to look real long enough for you to click, pay, reply, download, approve, or share.

So the new rule is simple: when money, identity, passwords, business access, payroll, legal threats, or urgency are involved, do not trust the message. Verify outside the message.

In the modern world, legitimacy is not something you assume. It is something you prove.

A scam does not need to look fake to be fake; it only needs to look real long enough for you to act.

Chapter 9

When Your Email Becomes the Front Door

Email is not just where messages arrive.

That is the first mistake people make. They treat email like a mailbox, as if it is only a place where communication lands. They think about spam, newsletters, bills, receipts, work messages, family updates, password resets, and calendar invitations. They think about email as a tool they use every day, so familiar that it almost feels boring.

But email is not boring to criminals.

Email is the front door. It is the master key. It is the recovery desk. It is the filing cabinet. It is the identity checkpoint. It is the business memory system. It is where banks send alerts, where payroll systems send notices, where cloud accounts send links, where social media platforms send recovery messages, where vendors send invoices, where clients send records, where contracts are exchanged, and where years of business decisions are documented.

That is why criminals want it.

If someone controls your email, they may not need to break into everything else directly. They can ask the rest of your life to let them in. They can reset passwords, watch conversations, intercept warnings, impersonate you, study your business, redirect money, and quietly wait for the perfect moment to act.

That is the part people underestimate. A compromised email account is not only an inbox problem. It can become an identity problem, a banking problem, a payroll problem, a vendor problem, a customer problem, a legal problem, and a reputation problem at the same time.

Most people think email security means avoiding suspicious messages. That matters, but it is only part of the picture. Email security is also about protecting the account that controls your other accounts. It is about protecting the place where password resets arrive. It is about protecting the history of your business relationships. It is about protecting the messages that prove who you are and what you own.

An inbox can contain years of identity, money, relationships, and proof.

That makes it valuable.

Think about what lives in the average inbox. Password reset links. Bank alerts. Invoices. Vendor communication. Client records. Contracts. Tax documents. Employee information. Business conversations. Social media recovery messages. Cloud storage links. Identity verification codes. Legal documents. Payroll records. Insurance information. Travel plans. Photos of documents. Old attachments. Account numbers. Receipts. Support tickets. Calendar invites. Private conversations.

Email is not one account.

Email is the map to many accounts.

That is why an attacker who gets into email can do more than read. They can study. They can search. They can learn which bank you use, which vendors you pay, which clients you serve, which employees report to you, which systems send alerts, which platforms are connected, and which relationships can be exploited. They can look for words like invoice, wire, payroll, password, contract, tax, payment, vendor, bank, login, code, document, and urgent.

They do not need to guess how your life or business works if your inbox explains it to them.

Once inside, criminals can also learn how you communicate. They can read old conversations. They can study your tone, timing, signatures, attachments, approval patterns, and business language. They can learn whether you are formal or casual, whether your employees expect short replies, whether vendors send monthly invoices, whether a certain client pays late, whether payroll is handled on a specific day, and whether your team is used to last-minute requests.

That makes impersonation more convincing.

They do not have to guess how you speak. They can read how you speak.

This is why a compromised email account can be more dangerous than an account that merely looks similar. A fake email address can fool people if they are not paying attention. But a real email account that has been taken over can fool people because the message comes from the place they already trust. The criminal does not have to create credibility from nothing. They inherit it.

For a business owner, this is extremely dangerous.

A business owner's email may be tied to banking, payroll, vendor decisions, client relationships, admin accounts, legal documents, domain records, cloud storage, social media pages, tax information, employee issues, contracts, and business strategy. In the wrong hands, that inbox becomes a command post.

A criminal can study vendors. Watch invoices. Send fake payment changes. Contact employees. Reset accounts. Access documents. Impersonate the owner. Hijack client trust. Delete warnings. Forward messages secretly. Monitor payroll timing. Watch contract negotiations. Learn who approves payments. Trigger account recovery flows. Damage reputation.

That is not a message problem. That is a business-control problem.

Owner email compromise can turn into a finance problem, an employee problem, a vendor problem, a client problem, and a legal problem before the owner even knows someone else is inside the account.

Employee email matters too. A criminal does not always need the owner's inbox first. One employee inbox can become a hallway into the business. It may contain login links, shared documents, customer conversations, vendor updates, internal files, payroll messages, calendar invites, HR notices, support tickets, approval requests, and clues about how the company operates.

The employee may not control the whole company. But their inbox may reveal how the company works.

That can be enough for a criminal to move deeper.

This is where business email compromise becomes one of the most serious threats facing modern organizations. In plain English, business email compromise is when criminals use email access, spoofing, or impersonation to trick a business into sending money, changing payment details, sharing information, or granting access.

It is not always a fake-looking email. Sometimes it is a real account being used for a criminal purpose. That is what makes it so dangerous.

Picture a vendor whose email account gets compromised. The attacker does not send a message immediately. They read. They study months of invoice conversations. They learn the vendor's language, billing timing, normal contact person, invoice style, payment schedule, and relationship with the customer.

Then they wait.

When payment is due, they send updated banking instructions inside the same conversation thread. The bookkeeper sees the real thread, the familiar vendor name, the correct invoice context, and professional wording. Nothing feels dramatic. Nothing screams cyberattack. It looks like normal business.

The payment is sent.

The real vendor never receives it.

Now the business has paid the criminal, still owes the vendor, and must prove what happened. That one email has become a banking issue, a vendor issue, an insurance issue, a legal issue, and a trust issue.

That is why email compromise is not just an inbox issue. It is a money issue.

It is also an identity issue. Email often contains enough personal information to help someone become you. An inbox may include your full name, address, phone number, date of birth, tax forms, insurance documents, bank names, employer information, family names, travel plans, account numbers, photos of identification, legal documents, medical or benefit information, and password reset messages.

Identity theft does not always start with one big file. Sometimes it starts with pieces collected from years of email.

That is why account recovery matters. Many systems treat email as proof of identity. If you control the email, you can often request a password reset, receive recovery codes, approve login changes, reset social media access, recover cloud accounts, or intercept security warnings.

Email control can become account control.

This is why email should be protected like a master key.

The problem is that many people protect email like it is ordinary. They use weak passwords. They reuse passwords. They do not turn on multi-factor authentication. They use personal email for business. They share inboxes with no controls. They leave old recovery emails attached. They never review forwarding rules. They click password reset links from messages. They use email as permanent file storage. They never check login history. They stay logged in on old devices. They forget to remove former employees. They let finance or payroll use the same weak protections as normal communication.

Email convenience becomes dangerous when it replaces control.

One of the most overlooked risks is the hidden forwarding rule. Attackers may create rules so copies of your emails go to them automatically. They may forward messages with certain words, archive security alerts, delete warnings, or move bank emails out of sight. That means they may keep watching even after the obvious problem seems fixed.

A person may change the password and believe the account is secure. But if forwarding rules, connected apps, active sessions, or recovery settings remain compromised, the attacker may still have visibility or a path back in.

Changing the password is not always cleaning the house. Sometimes it is only locking the front door while the back window is still open.

Criminals know how to hide inside email. They may delete alerts. Create inbox rules. Archive messages. Forward emails. Mark messages as read. Change recovery details. Add connected apps. Watch payment timing. Search old attachments. Monitor vendor conversations. Remove warnings from banks or platforms. Hide inside existing email threads. Wait before acting.

The scariest attacker is not always loud.

Sometimes they are patient.

That patience is what makes email compromise so damaging. A criminal who gets into an inbox may not act while the victim is watching closely. They may wait for a payment deadline. A trip. A contract negotiation. A payroll date. A customer dispute. A vendor renewal. A crisis. They wait until the request they want to make feels normal.

Then the message lands at exactly the wrong moment for the victim and exactly the right moment for the attacker.

This is why warning signs matter, but they are not always obvious. Some signs include missing emails, password reset alerts, sent messages you did not send, forwarding rules you did not create, login alerts, contacts receiving strange messages, emails marked read, unfamiliar devices, changed recovery information, bank or vendor messages you did not initiate, deleted security alerts, unusual archive activity, multi-factor prompts you did not request, new connected apps, or strange filters and mailbox rules.

But the absence of chaos does not mean the account is safe.

Some criminals hide quietly.

For business owners, the lesson is clear: do not treat every inbox equally. Owner, finance, payroll, admin, HR, legal, vendor-facing, and customer-support accounts need stronger controls because they sit closer to money, identity, authority, and trust.

That means stronger authentication. Access reviews. No shared passwords. No unapproved forwarding. Clear payment-change verification. Separate approval rules for money movement. Immediate lockout for former employees. Login monitoring. Domain protection. Evidence preservation. Secure recovery settings.

The accounts closest to money, identity, and authority need the strongest protection.

Businesses also need to understand the role of the email domain. A professional domain email is better for business operations than running a company through one free personal account. It builds credibility, separates personal and business identity, and gives the organization more control. But the domain itself must be protected.

Domain admin access, DNS settings, recovery email, registrar login, SPF, DKIM, DMARC, and administrator accounts matter. If criminals take over the domain or successfully spoof it, they can damage trust at scale. Your domain is part of your business identity. It is the digital version of your sign on the building, your letterhead, and the key to your office.

Protect it like all three.

Free email accounts are not automatically bad. The problem is concentration of risk. If one free email account controls banking, family accounts, social media, business tools, password resets, tax documents, job applications, cloud storage, and recovery access, then one account has become too powerful.

The danger is not the price.

The danger is putting everything behind one door.

That is true for individuals and businesses. A person may have one email tied to banking, medical records, children's school accounts, shopping, travel, insurance, taxes, social media, and work. A small business may have one owner's email tied to invoices, payroll, domain access, vendors, customer messages, cloud storage, social media, and payment systems. In both cases, the account becomes a control center.

Security must match the power of the account.

If an inbox controls money, identity, access, or recovery, it deserves more protection than a random newsletter account. The more an email account can control, the more protection it needs.

The practical steps are not complicated, but they must be taken seriously. Use a unique strong password. Use a password manager. Turn on multi-factor authentication, preferably with an authenticator app or passkey instead of relying only on text messages. Review the recovery email and phone number. Check forwarding rules. Check connected apps. Check login sessions. Log out unknown devices. Separate personal and business email. Stop using email as permanent storage for sensitive documents. Use secure cloud storage for sensitive files. Train employees. Lock former employees out immediately. Watch for password reset alerts. Protect the email accounts tied to banking, payroll, and admin systems most aggressively.

That list may sound basic, but basic controls prevent many serious problems. The issue is not that people have no options. The issue is that email has become so ordinary that people forget how much power it has.

If you suspect your email has been compromised, do not panic. Panic creates more mistakes. Use a safe device. Change the password. Enable or reset multi-factor authentication. Check recovery email and phone. Remove forwarding rules. Remove unknown connected apps. Log out all sessions. Check sent, deleted, archive, and rules. Check login history. Warn contacts if messages were sent. Review financial and vendor messages. Preserve evidence. Report internally if the issue is business-related. Watch for follow-up attacks. Check every important account connected to that email.

Do not only change the password.

Clean the house.

That phrase matters because many people treat account recovery as a single action. They regain access and assume the problem is over. But if the attacker had time inside the account, you have to assume they may have changed settings, read sensitive information, searched for financial relationships, copied documents, created forwarding rules, connected apps, or used the inbox to reset other accounts.

Recovery should include investigation, not just access restoration.

For a business, that investigation should be documented. What account was affected? When did unusual access begin? What messages were sent? Were vendor or payroll conversations touched? Were payments changed? Were clients contacted? Were forwarding rules created? Were security alerts deleted? What accounts use this email for recovery? What evidence needs to be preserved? Who must be notified? What controls need to change so this does not happen again?

Those are leadership questions, not just technical questions.

A strong cybersecurity program should treat email as a control center, not a message box. It should flag suspicious login behavior. Watch for unusual forwarding rules. Help review active sessions. Recommend stronger authentication. Identify messages involving invoices, payroll, vendor changes, legal threats, identity, and access. Preserve evidence when risk is meaningful. Explain the problem in plain English. Help the user verify before acting. Log what happened so the business has a timeline instead of scattered memories.

That is where the future of protection has to go. It cannot only say, 'This email looks suspicious.' It has to ask: what does this inbox control? Is this message trying to move money? Is it changing payment instructions? Is it asking for credentials? Is it inside an old thread? Is the sender a real account being misused? Are there unfamiliar sessions? Has recovery information changed? Is someone being pushed to bypass normal approval?

Email risk is not only about content. It is about control.

If your email controls password resets, then email is part of identity security. If it controls vendor payments, then email is part of financial security. If it controls payroll, then email is part of employee security. If it controls customer communication, then email is part of reputation security. If it controls admin access, then email is part of operational security.

That is why email is the front door.

It is not the only door, but it is one of the most important. And too many people leave it protected by a reused password, an old recovery phone number, no authentication, unknown forwarding rules, and years of sensitive information sitting in folders no one reviews.

That has to change.

Protecting email is not optional anymore. Not for individuals. Not for families. Not for business owners. Not for employees who handle customers, vendors, payroll, money, legal documents, or access. The inbox is where criminals look for the keys to everything else.

So treat it that way.

Do not treat email like a junk drawer for your digital life. Do not let one account control everything without stronger protection. Do not assume that because you can still log in, no one else has been there. Do not assume that changing a password removes every trace of compromise. Do not assume that an email from a familiar account is safe just because the address is real.

Protect the account. Review the settings. Control the recovery paths. Watch the sessions. Verify the requests. Preserve the evidence. Train the people. Lock the doors you forgot were doors.

Your inbox is not just a place where messages arrive. It is one of the main control centers of your identity and business.

Protect your email like a front door, a safe, and a master key, because in the wrong hands, it can become all three.

Chapter 10

Passwords, Phones, and the Keys to Your Life

People say, "It is just a password."

No. It is not just a password.

That password may unlock your email. Your email may reset your bank. Your phone may approve the code. Your cloud account may hold your tax records. Your social media may control your reputation. Your payroll system may control your employees' money. Your domain account may control your business identity.

One weak password can become a hallway.

One compromised phone can become a master key.

That is why this chapter matters. Passwords and phones are not small security details anymore. They are part of the identity system that holds modern life together. They connect to money, business, family, reputation, cloud files, employee records, payroll, social media, banking, insurance, taxes, and recovery. If the wrong person gets control of the password or the phone, they may not need to break every lock. They may already have the keys.

The keys to your life are no longer only on a key ring. They are in passwords, phones, recovery codes, sessions, and the accounts connected to them.

This is where many people make a dangerous mistake. They think of a password as one small thing attached to one account. But a password is rarely isolated. It may be connected to other accounts through email. It may be reused across personal and business systems. It may be saved in a browser. It may be stored in a screenshot, a note, an old chat, or an email. It may be known by a former employee. It may have been exposed years ago in a breach the owner barely remembers.

The issue is not only whether the password looks strong. The issue is where else that password has been used.

Password reuse is not a convenience problem. It is a chain-reaction problem.

If an old shopping site, game account, forum, or app gets breached, criminals may take that email and password combination and test it everywhere else. They may try email, banking, payroll, social media, cloud storage, shopping accounts, business software, tax accounts, insurance portals, and admin dashboards. The breach may happen in one place, but the damage may happen somewhere else.

That is the part people miss. They say, "That old account did not matter." Maybe the old account did not matter by itself. But the password mattered if it was reused. The email address mattered if it was connected to other accounts. The pattern mattered if it gave criminals a working key to try somewhere more valuable.

Credential stuffing is the plain-English name for this. Criminals take stolen usernames and passwords from one place and automatically try them everywhere else. They are not guessing. They are testing old keys in new doors.

That is why every important account needs its own unique password.

Not because cybersecurity professionals like making life harder. Because one reused password gives criminals a way to turn one breach into many attempts. If one password opens your old shopping account, your email, your business

That is a powerful convenience. It is also a serious risk. If the phone is compromised, stolen, unlocked, cloned, or the number is taken over, the attacker may be able to bypass the password entirely. They may receive codes. They may approve prompts. They may access apps already logged in. They may read texts, open email, view contacts, check documents, and reset accounts before the owner understands what is happening.

A phone-number takeover can be devastating. Through SIM swapping or port-out fraud, a criminal may move the victim's phone number to a device or account they control. Once that happens, they may receive verification codes, password reset messages, banking alerts, social media recovery links, and account notifications. Then they can race to reset accounts before the victim understands why their phone stopped working.

This is why phone carrier security matters. Most people think about their bank password, but not the account with their mobile carrier. Yet that carrier account may control the phone number that receives recovery codes for the bank. If the carrier account is weak, the phone number becomes easier to attack. If the phone number is taken over, other accounts may follow.

This is also why multi-factor authentication matters, but it has to be understood correctly. Many people believe multi-factor authentication makes them completely safe. It does not. It is important, but it is not magic.

Multi-factor authentication makes you harder to attack, but you still have to use the right kind and protect the recovery path.

Text-message codes are better than nothing, but they are weaker because they depend on the phone number. If the phone number is taken over, the codes may go to the attacker. Authenticator apps are stronger because they are not tied directly to the phone number. Passkeys and security keys are stronger where available because they are more resistant to phishing. Recovery codes are powerful and must be protected because they can bypass normal login controls.

software, and your payroll system, then the password is not one key. It is a master key you accidentally copied for every door.

The most dangerous accounts should be protected first. Email is at the top because email resets other accounts. Banking matters because it controls money. Payroll matters because it controls employee pay and sensitive records. Cloud storage matters because it holds documents. The phone carrier matters because the phone number may receive codes and recovery messages. Business admin accounts matter because they can change settings, invite users, remove controls, or access company data.

Social media matters because it controls reputation. A domain registrar matters because it controls the business identity online. Accounting software matters because it reveals money movement. A password manager matters because it protects the keys. Tax accounts, insurance portals, payment processors, legal document systems, HR systems, and vendor platforms all matter because each one touches identity, money, records, or trust.

The rule is simple: the account that can reset other accounts is more dangerous than it looks.

That is why the phone becomes part of password security. The phone has become part of identity. It may hold text-message codes, authenticator apps, banking apps, email access, social media accounts, password reset prompts, business tools, cloud files, contacts, recovery codes, mobile wallets, device approvals, and login notifications.

For many people, the phone is now the master key.

It unlocks accounts. It receives codes. It approves logins. It stores apps. It receives bank alerts. It recovers social media. It holds business conversations. It may control payroll, email, identity, and admin access.

In the last chapter, we treated email as the front door. The phone is the key in your pocket.

The strongest protection should go on the accounts that control money, identity, admin access, email, payroll, and recovery. Not every account carries the same risk. A recipe website and a payroll account do not deserve the same level of urgency. The accounts closest to money, identity, and authority need the strongest protection.

People also weaken multi-factor authentication by accident. They share codes. They type codes into fake websites. They approve login prompts they did not request. They store recovery codes in email. They use the same compromised phone for every account. They leave old devices logged in. They keep old recovery numbers attached. They use weak recovery questions. They let former employees keep access. They ignore login alerts because they are busy.

A login prompt you did not request is not an inconvenience. It is a warning.

That line matters. If your phone asks you to approve a login and you are not trying to log in, do not approve it just to make the notification go away. Someone may be trying to get in. If you receive a code you did not request, do not share it with anyone. If someone calls and says they need the code to verify you, stop. Codes are keys. Treat them that way.

This is where password managers become practical protection. People cannot realistically memorize a different strong password for every account in modern life. That is not a character flaw. It is a math problem. The average person has too many accounts. A business owner has even more. A password manager helps create and store unique strong passwords so security is not built around memory.

Do not build your security around memory. Build it around unique passwords, stronger authentication, and recovery control.

Browser-saved passwords are another area where people need nuance. They are convenient, and convenience matters. But people need to understand the tradeoff. If the device, browser profile, synced account, or main computer login is compromised, stored passwords may become part of the damage. That does not mean every person must panic and immediately stop using browser storage for every account. It means important accounts deserve stronger handling, especially email, banking, payroll, admin dashboards, domain registrars, tax portals, and password managers.

Convenience should never be confused with control.

For normal people, the password rule should be simple. Every important account needs a unique password. Your email password should never be reused. Your banking password should never be reused. Your business passwords should never be shared. Your password manager password should be unique and strong. Your admin accounts should have the strongest protection. Use a password manager instead of memory.

The phone rule should be just as simple. Lock your phone. Update it. Review your apps. Protect your phone carrier account. Do not share codes. Do not approve login prompts you did not request. Remove old devices. Use authenticator apps or passkeys where possible. Separate personal and business access where possible. Do not keep recovery codes sitting in email, screenshots, or unsecured notes.

Your phone is not just a device. It is part of your identity system.

Inside a business, passwords and phones become business risk. Personal habits can control company systems. An employee reuses a password. A business owner's phone gets compromised. A payroll code gets intercepted. A shared password is leaked. A former employee still has access. A personal phone controls company accounts. An old admin account remains active. A password is saved in a browser on a shared device. A phone number tied to payroll gets taken over. A finance login uses text-message codes only. A contractor keeps access after the project ends.

Those are not private preferences anymore. They are business controls.

A business can have good intentions and still create risk if passwords and phones are not managed. Shared passwords may feel easier until someone leaves the company. Personal phones may feel convenient until one phone becomes the recovery path for critical accounts. Old admin access may feel harmless until it is used. A weak recovery email may feel insignificant until it resets the system that controls payroll.

The problem is not one bad habit. The problem is connected habits.

Here is a simple example. A small business owner reused an old password from a shopping account. That shopping site was breached years ago. The owner forgot the password was reused. Criminals test the same email and password against the owner's email account. It works.

Now they can see invoices, payroll alerts, client messages, tax documents, password resets, and business software notifications. Then they try to reset the business bank account. The reset code goes to the owner's phone. If they can trick the owner into sharing it, or if they can take over the phone number, they may control the account.

The mistake started as "just a reused password." It became access to the business.

That is how these attacks grow. They begin with one weak place and move toward a stronger prize. The old password opens the email. The email reveals the bank. The phone receives the code. The cloud folder holds documents. The social media account controls reputation. The payroll system controls money. The domain account controls the business identity. The attacker follows the connections.

This is why business owners need structure. Ban shared passwords for critical systems. Require multi-factor authentication. Use a password manager. Remove former employees immediately. Review admin accounts regularly. Protect owner, finance, payroll, and HR phones. Separate personal and business accounts. Use role-based access. Store recovery codes securely. Train employees not to share codes. Review active sessions. Protect the domain registrar. Protect accounting software. Protect payment processors. Require verification for payment, payroll, vendor, and admin changes.

The accounts closest to money, identity, payroll, and authority need the strongest protection.

That means the owner cannot treat their own phone casually. The owner phone may approve banking, payroll, social media, domain changes, vendor payments, and account resets. The finance phone may receive codes tied to money movement. The HR phone may connect to employee records. The admin account may control everything behind the scenes. These are not ordinary devices and accounts. They are high-value keys.

A company should also know what happens when someone leaves. Former employees should not keep access because removing them is inconvenient. Contractors should not keep credentials because no one remembered to revoke them. Shared passwords should not survive staff changes. Recovery codes should not sit in an old email account that no one checks. Devices should not stay logged in indefinitely.

Offboarding is security. Access review is security. Device review is security. Recovery-code storage is security. These are not extra tasks. They are how a business protects the keys.

If a password may be compromised, act from a safe device. Change the password. Log out all sessions. Enable or reset multi-factor authentication. Check recovery settings. Remove unknown devices. Check email, bank, and cloud activity. Review other accounts using the same password. Preserve evidence. Notify business contacts if relevant. Watch for follow-up attacks.

If a phone number may be compromised, contact the phone carrier immediately. Lock the carrier account. Check for SIM swap or port-out activity. Review bank and email access. Change passwords from a safe device. Reset multi-factor authentication. Move away from text-message authentication where possible. Check social media recovery settings. Watch for follow-up scams.

Do not only change one password. Assume connected accounts may also be at risk.

That is the difference between reacting to one symptom and cleaning the system. If the password was reused, every account using that password needs attention. If the phone was taken over, every account that used that phone for recovery needs attention. If a session was stolen, changing the password may not be enough until old sessions are revoked. If recovery settings were changed, the attacker may still have a path back in.

This is why a strong cybersecurity program should treat passwords, phones, sessions, recovery codes, and account recovery as one connected identity system. It should ask whether a password was reused, whether the account is tied to banking or payroll, whether the phone number controls recovery, whether authentication is text-only, whether unfamiliar sessions exist, whether former employees are still active, whether personal phones control company access, whether repeated login attempts are happening, and whether a high-risk action followed a password or phone event.

A real protection system should be able to revoke sessions, force password resets, trigger stronger authentication, freeze sensitive actions, hold payroll or vendor changes, alert the owner or administrator, preserve evidence, review recovery settings, remove unknown devices, recommend stronger authentication, and log what happened. The point is not to create more noise. The point is to protect the keys before one weak key opens too many doors.

For individuals, the lesson is personal. For businesses, the lesson is operational. The same password mistake that embarrasses a person can financially damage a company. The same phone takeover that locks a person out of social media can redirect payroll, hijack vendor payments, or expose customer records if that phone controls business access.

We cannot keep separating personal behavior from business security when personal devices and personal habits control business systems.

That does not mean every employee is the enemy. It means every employee needs a safe way to handle keys. They need rules. They need tools. They need training. They need a way to report suspicious prompts. They need to know that they should never share codes, never reuse passwords for business systems, never keep company credentials in personal notes, and never approve a login they did not request.

Security should make the right behavior easier than the risky behavior.

The average person does not need to become an expert in encryption, authentication protocols, or identity architecture to make better decisions. They need to understand the basic truth: passwords, phones, and recovery paths are connected. If one is weak, the others can be used against you.

So start with the accounts that matter most. Protect email. Protect banking. Protect payroll. Protect cloud storage. Protect business admin accounts. Protect the phone carrier account. Protect the domain registrar. Protect the password manager. Protect the accounts that can reset other accounts. Then work outward.

Do not wait for the perfect system. Close the obvious doors first.

Use unique passwords. Turn on stronger authentication. Stop sharing codes. Remove old devices. Review recovery settings. Lock your phone. Protect your carrier account. Separate personal and business accounts where possible. Remove former employees. Preserve evidence when something goes wrong. Treat unusual login prompts as warnings, not annoyances.

These steps may sound simple. They are simple. That is why they matter. Cybersecurity fails when people ignore simple controls because they are waiting for complicated solutions. Criminals love the basics because the basics are where people get lazy.

A weak password is basic. A reused password is basic. An unprotected phone number is basic. An old device session is basic. A former employee account is basic. A recovery code in an email folder is basic. But basic does not mean harmless. Basic failures can create serious damage.

The keys to your life are no longer only on a key ring. They are in your passwords, your phone, your recovery codes, and the accounts connected to them.

Protect the password. Protect the phone. Protect the keys.

Because in the digital world, whoever holds the keys can start opening doors.

Chapter 11

Social Engineering: The Hack That Starts With Trust

Many cyberattacks do not begin with code.

They begin with trust.

That is the part people miss. They imagine cybersecurity as a battle between a criminal and a machine. They picture passwords being guessed, networks being scanned, firewalls being tested, and malicious code trying to force its way through a system. Those attacks exist, but many of the most damaging incidents begin somewhere much more ordinary.

They begin with a message that feels familiar. A phone call that sounds official. A request that appears to come from the boss. A vendor update that looks routine. A family member who seems to need help. A customer complaint that demands attention. A fake opportunity that arrives at exactly the right emotional moment.

The easiest system to hack is often not the computer. It is the person who trusts the wrong signal at the wrong time.

That is social engineering.

Social engineering is when someone manipulates human trust to get access, information, money, or action. They may pretend to be a bank, a boss, a vendor, a family member, a customer, an investor, an attorney, a platform support team, a charity, a government agency, a recruiter, or a friend. They are not only attacking your device. They are attacking your decision.

This is why social engineering is so dangerous. It does not require the victim to be foolish. It requires the right pressure at the wrong moment.

People often think social engineering only works on gullible people. That is wrong. It works on busy people. Smart people. Helpful people. Trusting people. Distracted people. Overwhelmed people. Professional people. People who do not want to disappoint someone. People who are trying to solve a problem quickly. People who are trying to be polite. People who are trying to protect someone they care about.

Social engineering does not require stupidity. It requires a human being under pressure.

That is why we have to stop shaming victims. Shame makes people hide mistakes. Shame makes employees delay reporting suspicious messages. Shame makes parents feel embarrassed. Shame makes business owners keep quiet too long. And silence helps criminals. Reporting helps everyone.

A strong cybersecurity culture does not begin by calling people careless. It begins by understanding how people actually behave when they are under stress. The attacker studies that behavior. They study pressure, habits, emotion, authority, fear, urgency, helpfulness, confusion, loneliness, hope, loyalty, and the need to respond.

The attacker studies what makes people move.

Trust is powerful because trust lowers defenses. If a message appears to come from your boss, you move faster. If it appears to come from your bank, you worry. If it appears to come from your child, you panic. If it appears to come from a vendor, you process it. If it appears to come from a client, you respond. If it appears to come from a public figure, church, nonprofit, employer, or government agency, you may assume authority before you verify identity.

Criminals do not always need you to trust them. They need you to trust the name they are wearing.

That is the heart of social engineering. The criminal borrows trust from someone or something already familiar to you. They borrow the bank's authority. The boss's urgency. The vendor's relationship. The child's emotional pull. The client's importance. The attorney's seriousness. The platform's brand. The government's weight. Then they use that borrowed trust to push you toward action.

They may not even need you to believe the whole story. They only need you to act before you slow down enough to test it.

The emotions they use are not random. Fear is powerful. Urgency is powerful. Greed can be powerful. Hope is powerful. Loneliness is powerful. Helpfulness is powerful. Embarrassment is powerful. Authority is powerful. Confusion is powerful. Sympathy is powerful. Opportunity is powerful. Loyalty is powerful.

They do not always need to scare you. Sometimes they need you to care.

A fake charity request works because someone cares. A romance scam works because someone wants connection. A fake job offer works because someone needs opportunity. A fake message from a child works because a parent wants to protect. A fake vendor request works because a business wants to honor its obligations. A fake customer complaint works because a company wants to respond professionally. A fake boss message works because an employee wants to be useful.

Social engineering abuses good intentions.

That is why the most dangerous emotion in cybersecurity may be urgency. Fear is powerful. Hope is powerful. Helpfulness is powerful. Trust is powerful. But urgency is the accelerator. Urgency makes people skip verification. Urgency makes smart people rush. Urgency makes normal processes feel too slow. Urgency makes doubt feel irresponsible.

So here is the rule: when pressure goes up, speed goes down.

That line should be remembered by every employee, every parent, every business owner, every executive, and every person who uses a phone. When someone pressures you to act faster than you can verify, the answer is not to move faster. The answer is to slow down. Pressure is not proof. Urgency is not authority. A deadline is not identity. A threat is not verification.

Social engineering shows up in everyday life in ways that look ordinary. A text appears to come from a child or family member asking for help. A bank alert says your account is locked. A vendor asks for updated payment information. A person builds a romantic relationship and later asks for money. A job offer requests personal documents. An investment opportunity promises a special opening. A charity request uses tragedy. A customer complaint demands a quick response. A fake boss message asks for gift cards, payments, or confidential information. A tech-support call says your computer has a problem.

The scam does not always arrive wearing a mask. Sometimes it arrives wearing a familiar name.

Inside a business, social engineering becomes even more dangerous because people are trained to respond. Work is built around responsiveness. Customers need answers. Vendors need payments. Payroll needs accuracy. Owners need support. Executives need things done quickly. Employees do not want to be the person who slowed everything down.

That is exactly what criminals exploit.

An employee receives an urgent owner request. A bookkeeper receives a payment-change email. HR receives a fake employee update. A vendor asks for new banking details. A fake client asks for sensitive documents. A caller pressures staff for information. A fake legal notice scares the team into action. A fake customer complaint creates panic. A fake executive message pushes payroll or finance to act. A fake job applicant sends a malicious attachment.

Business social engineering is not just a scam. It is an attack on workflow.

That distinction matters. If we only ask whether the message looks suspicious, we miss what the message is trying to do. Is it trying to move money? Change access? Capture identity? Bypass approval? Create secrecy? Trigger fear? Exploit helpfulness? Force an employee to act alone? If the answer is yes, the message deserves more scrutiny, even if it looks normal.

Social engineering often happens before the technical attack. First, criminals collect information. They watch social media. They study public posts. They learn names. They copy writing styles. They build fake profiles. They create fake documents. They learn relationships. They learn what matters to the person or business. Then they use that information to create trust, pressure, and action.

The hack may begin before anyone clicks anything.

Social media makes this easier because social media gives criminals research material. People reveal family details, travel plans, workplaces, job titles, events, friends, vendors, causes, political views, fears, habits, photos, relationships, business goals, recent purchases, new jobs, new clients, grief, excitement, and public pressure points. A criminal can use that information to make a message feel personal, timely, and believable.

A fake message that says, “I saw you were traveling this week,” feels different from a random scam. A message that references a real event feels different. A fake vendor request that arrives after the company publicly thanks that vendor feels different. A fake customer complaint that references a real product feels different. Personal information does not have to be secret to be useful. It only has to make the lie feel closer to the truth.

Artificial intelligence makes this worse because it makes manipulation faster and more convincing. AI can help create fake voices, fake videos, more personal messages, better scripts, fake profiles, fake documents, fake emotional tone, more convincing romance scams, fake executive messages, AI-written business emails, fake customer support, fake legal threats, fake job applications, and fake investment pitches.

AI helps criminals scale empathy, pressure, and impersonation.

That should concern people. A fake voice does not matter only because it is technologically impressive. It matters because it hijacks trust. A fake video does not matter only because it looks interesting. It matters because it can make authority appear real. A fake executive message does not matter only because it is polished. It matters because someone may act before they verify. We will go deeper into deepfakes later, but for now, understand this: deepfakes are not only a technology issue. They are social engineering with a stronger costume.

Another major danger is verification theater. Verification theater is when scammers create enough fake process to make doubt feel unreasonable. They may provide paperwork, fake websites, fake references, fake reviews, fake business names, fake contracts, fake dashboards, fake phone numbers, fake customer service, fake badges, and fake approval steps. It feels legitimate because it has structure.

But structure is not proof.

A scam can have paperwork. A scam can have a process. A scam can have a website. A scam can have people answering phones. A scam can have forms, signatures, contracts, portals, and professional language. Verification theater is the stage built around the lie.

This is one of the reasons scams can fool capable people. The victim is not always ignoring red flags. Sometimes the scam is designed to manufacture green flags. It gives the victim enough official-looking information to make suspicion feel unreasonable. It creates a world where every step appears to confirm the last step. Then it pressures the victim to act before they step outside that world and verify independently.

That is why independent verification matters. If the proof only exists inside the system controlled by the person making the request, it is not enough.

Authority is another tool criminals use well. They borrow authority to make people obey. They may say, “This is your bank.” “This is the IRS.” “This is your boss.” “This is your attorney.” “This is law enforcement.” “This is payroll.” “This is your platform support team.” “This is your investor.” “This is your vendor.” “This is your insurance provider.” “This is your school.” “This is your church.” “This is your client.”

Authority makes the request feel bigger than the person receiving it. That is the trap. A person who would normally ask questions may stop asking because the title feels too important. An employee who would normally verify may skip verification because the message appears to come from leadership. A parent may obey because the message appears to involve a child. A customer may comply because the message appears to come from the platform they already use.

Secrecy is another warning sign. Secrecy isolates the victim. Scammers say, “Do not tell anyone.” “This is confidential.” “This must stay between us.” “Do not contact your bank.” “Do not involve your team.” “Your account will be locked if you delay.” “You will lose the opportunity if you ask questions.” “This is a private matter.” “You cannot discuss this yet.”

Real safety does not usually require isolation.

If someone is pressuring you to keep the request secret, especially when money, identity, access, payroll, legal pressure, or personal safety is involved, slow down. Secrecy removes the people who might protect you. That is why criminals use it.

Helpfulness may be the hardest one to talk about because it is not a bad trait. People want to help. They want to solve the problem. They want to respond quickly. They want to protect someone. They want to be professional. They want to not disappoint the boss. They want to help the customer. They want to support the family member. They want to be polite. They want to be useful.

Social engineering turns those good instincts into entry points.

That is why organizations need no-shame reporting. An employee should never feel punished for saying, "This request feels off." A bookkeeper should be allowed to slow down a payment. A receptionist should be allowed to refuse a caller asking for internal information. An assistant should be allowed to verify an executive request outside the message. A customer service person should be allowed to escalate a strange complaint. The fastest way to make a business vulnerable is to punish people for slowing down.

A safe culture makes verification normal.

There are warning signs of social engineering. Unusual urgency. Pressure to act alone. Secrecy. Changed payment details. Requests for passwords or codes. Emotional manipulation. A new communication channel. Refusal to verify another way. A too-good-to-be-true opportunity. Fear of consequences. A request to bypass normal process. An unusual authority claim. An unexpected attachment. A request for gift cards, wire transfer, crypto, or urgent payment. Something that feels almost normal but not quite.

The feeling of pressure is itself a signal.

When pressure goes up, speed goes down.

If someone pressures you to act faster than you can verify, slow down. Do not argue. Do not panic. Do not rush. Do not click. Do not pay. Do not send codes. Do not keep it secret. Pause and verify through a separate trusted channel.

Business owners should train employees to do the same thing. Pause. Verify through known channels. Escalate unusual requests. Never share codes. Never bypass payment rules. Report suspicious pressure. Ask, "Is this normal for this relationship?" Preserve evidence. Slow down money movement. Confirm vendor changes outside email. Confirm executive requests outside the message. Never punish employees for asking questions.

That last part matters. If employees think asking questions will make them look incompetent, they will stop asking. If they think leadership values speed over accuracy every time, they will move quickly even when the request deserves caution. If they think reporting a suspicious message creates trouble for them, they will delete it and hope nothing happens.

That is not security. That is silence.

A business that wants to defend against social engineering needs a trust test. Before money moves, before access changes, before identity information is shared, before payroll is altered, before a legal threat triggers panic, ask the right questions.

Is this person who they claim to be? Is this channel normal? Is the request normal? Is the timing suspicious? Is urgency being manufactured? Can I verify outside this message? Am I being asked for money, identity, access, or secrecy? Am I being asked to bypass normal process? Would I still trust this if I removed the logo, title, or emotional pressure? Who benefits if I act immediately?

This is not paranoia. This is disciplined trust.

Disciplined trust is different from distrust. Distrust assumes everyone is lying. Disciplined trust says trust is valuable enough to protect with verification. It allows relationships to function while preventing criminals from borrowing those relationships unchecked.

For families, disciplined trust may mean calling the child back through a known number. For individuals, it may mean going directly to the bank app instead of clicking the link. For businesses, it may mean verifying vendor banking changes through a known contact. For employees, it may mean confirming an executive request through a separate channel. For leaders, it may mean building approval gates around risky actions.

A strong protection program should treat social engineering as a human-trust attack. It should not only ask, "Is this link dangerous?" It should ask: what trust is being borrowed? What emotion is being triggered? Is urgency being manufactured? Is secrecy being requested? Is authority being claimed? Is helpfulness being exploited? Is the request normal for this relationship? Is money, identity, access, payroll, legal pressure, or business authority involved? Is the user being asked to bypass normal approval? Does the evidence prove legitimacy, or only appearance?

Those questions move cybersecurity closer to the real attack. The attacker is not always trying to defeat the computer first. Sometimes the attacker is trying to defeat the decision. So the defense has to protect the decision.

That may mean a payment hold when vendor information changes. A callback through a known channel. A second approval for payroll or banking changes. Evidence capture when a suspicious request arrives. An incident timeline when pressure repeats. Fake-profile tracking when impersonation appears. Deepfake escalation when voice or video is involved. Plain-English warnings that explain not only that something is risky, but why it is risky.

The goal is not to make people afraid of every message. The goal is to help people recognize when trust is being used as a tool against them.

Social engineering works because it attacks the human need to trust, help, respond, and belong. The defense is not paranoia. The defense is verification.

You do not have to stop trusting people. You do have to stop letting pressure replace proof. You do not have to become suspicious of every relationship. You do have to understand that criminals borrow real relationships to create fake authority. You do not have to live afraid. You do have to make verification part of how you protect yourself and your business.

The easiest system to hack is often not the computer. It is the person who trusts the wrong signal at the wrong time. But once that person learns to pause, verify, and report without shame, the attack becomes much harder.

When someone pressures you to move faster than you can verify, slow down — because the pressure may be the attack.

Chapter 12

Ransomware, Account Takeovers, and Digital Hostage Situations

A digital hostage situation does not always mean your files are encrypted.

That is the first thing people need to understand. The old image of ransomware is a locked computer screen with a message demanding payment. That still happens. But the modern threat is broader than one frozen laptop or one encrypted folder. Sometimes the hostage is not the file. Sometimes the hostage is the account, the money, the identity, the reputation, the website, the phone number, the payroll system, the business page, the cloud storage, or the system you need to function.

The common thread is control.

Cybercriminals do not always need to destroy you. Sometimes they only need to lock you out, hold access, threaten exposure, interrupt operations, or force you to make decisions under pressure. They do not always need to burn the building down. Sometimes they only need to hold the keys and tell you what it will cost to get back inside.

That is why ransomware, account takeover, and digital extortion belong in the same conversation. They may look different on the surface, but underneath, they are all about leverage. Someone else controls something you need, and they use that control to create fear, urgency, and obedience.

Ransomware, in plain English, is when criminals lock, steal, or threaten your data or systems and demand payment or action before they release control or stop the damage. They take control of something you need, then use pressure to make you pay, obey, or panic.

But ransomware is only one version of a digital hostage situation. A locked email account can become a hostage situation. A hijacked social media account can become a hostage situation. A frozen payroll system can become a hostage situation. A stolen domain can become a hostage situation. A taken-over phone number can become a hostage situation. A cloud account that no longer belongs to you can become a hostage situation. A payment processor you cannot access can become a hostage situation. A customer database someone threatens to leak can become a hostage situation.

The question is not only, "Are the files encrypted?" The better question is, "What do we still control?"

That question changes everything.

For a long time, people thought of ransomware as a malware problem. Malware matters. Endpoint protection matters. Patching matters. Backups matter. But the real danger is not only encryption. The real danger is losing control. When someone else controls the systems, accounts, data, or reputation your business depends on, you are no longer dealing with a normal technical issue. You are dealing with a continuity event.

For a small business, that can become an existential event. For a larger organization, it can become a crisis of operations, legal exposure, customer trust, payroll, vendor confidence, and executive decision-making. For a family or individual, it can become panic, shame, identity loss, and the feeling that someone else has taken over part of your life.

That emotional side matters because criminals use it.

When people lose control, they often feel panic, embarrassment, anger, shame, confusion, helplessness, fear of customers finding out, fear of losing money, fear of not recovering, fear of looking irresponsible, fear of employees asking questions, and fear of the business failing. Those feelings are not weakness. They are human. But criminals know fear shortens thinking.

Panic is part of the attack surface.

The attacker wants you rushed. They want you isolated. They want you clicking, paying, deleting, reconnecting, posting, and explaining before you know what actually happened. They want you to make the crisis worse because you are trying to make it end faster.

That is why the first minutes matter.

The first job is not to fix everything. The first job is to stop making the situation worse.

When ransomware or account takeover appears, people may panic-click, delete evidence, pay too fast, change the wrong password, warn the attacker, keep using a compromised device, tell customers before knowing the facts, lock themselves out further, miss the real entry point, or assume one password change fixes everything. Every one of those reactions is understandable. Every one can also create more damage.

So the first response has to be disciplined.

Do not panic-click. Do not delete evidence. Do not immediately pay without professional, legal, insurance, or law-enforcement guidance where appropriate. Do not keep using a device you believe may be compromised. Do not argue with the attacker. Do not hide it from the business if business systems are involved. Do not assume one password change fixes everything. Do not contact customers publicly before knowing the facts. Do not reconnect infected systems too quickly. Do not use the compromised email account to coordinate recovery.

That last point is important. If the attacker controls the email, and you use that same email to plan recovery, you may be telling the attacker what you are doing. If they control a chat account, do not use that chat to coordinate response. If they control a phone number, do not rely on that number for recovery. One of the first questions in any serious incident should be: what communication channel is still clean?

A practical first response should follow a simple pattern: contain, preserve, verify, recover, communicate, and harden.

Contain means stop the spread. Stop using the compromised account or device. Disconnect an affected device or network segment if ransomware is suspected. Freeze sensitive actions if money, payroll, vendor payments, or admin access may be affected. Revoke suspicious sessions when it is safe to do so. Lock down accounts that control recovery.

Preserve means keep evidence before it disappears. Take screenshots. Save messages. Write down times, account names, devices, phone numbers, payment requests, file names, and what happened. Preserve emails, URLs, sender information, ransom notes, login alerts, platform notices, and transaction details. Evidence matters for banks, platforms, insurers, attorneys, investigators, and your own internal understanding of the incident.

Verify means confirm what is real. What account is actually compromised? What system is locked? What data may be stolen? What still works? What communication channels are trusted? What administrator accounts are still clean? What recovery paths still belong to you? Who has authority to make decisions? What must be isolated before anything else is touched?

Recover means restore control safely. Change passwords from a clean device. Enable or reset multi-factor authentication. Revoke sessions. Check recovery settings. Remove unknown forwarding rules, devices, connected apps, and admin accounts. Notify the bank, platform, phone carrier, domain registrar, or payment processor if needed. Contact IT or security support. Contact cyber insurance or legal counsel if applicable. Restore from known-good backups only after you understand the risk.

Communicate means speak carefully once you know enough. Internally, the right people need to know quickly. Externally, customers, vendors, regulators, insurers, platforms, or law enforcement may need to know depending on the facts. But communication should be controlled. Posting publicly while confused can create more damage. Saying too little can create mistrust. Saying too much before facts are known can create legal and reputation problems.

Harden means close the door that created the incident, and also close the doors the incident revealed. If a password was reused, fix the reuse problem. If a phone number was taken over, strengthen carrier security and move critical accounts away from text-message codes where possible. If ransomware reached shared files, review access and backups. If an account recovery path was changed, review every account connected to it. If a vendor process failed, add verification gates.

This is how a crisis becomes controlled instead of chaotic.

Account takeover deserves special attention because it can be just as damaging as ransomware. If someone takes over email, banking, payroll, social media, cloud storage, a domain registrar, a payment processor, website hosting, or an admin dashboard, they may control the business without encrypting a single file.

They can lock the real owner out. They can impersonate the company. They can redirect money. They can message customers. They can reset passwords. They can change recovery settings. They can delete warnings. They can damage reputation. They can hold access hostage. No ransom note is required for a business to be trapped.

The most dangerous accounts are the ones that control money, identity, access, reputation, or recovery. Email. Banking. Payroll. Social media. Cloud storage. Phone carrier. Domain registrar. Website hosting. Payment processors. Accounting systems. Admin dashboards. Customer databases. Password manager. Tax accounts. Insurance portals. CRM. Vendor portals. App stores and developer accounts.

Any account that can stop operations, move money, reset access, or speak publicly for the business is critical infrastructure.

That is not an exaggeration. If the business loses its domain, customers may not know what website or email address to trust. If it loses the payment processor, sales may stop. If it loses payroll, employees may not get paid. If it loses social media, the public voice of the company may be controlled by someone else. If it loses email, recovery for multiple systems may be at risk. If it loses the password manager, many other doors may be exposed.

A digital hostage situation can stop a business in practical ways. No access to files. Payroll delays. Vendor payments blocked. Customer communication stopped. Website down. Social media hijacked. Orders interrupted. Appointments lost. Employees waiting. Clients losing trust. Legal issues. Insurance issues. Regulatory exposure. Reputation damage. Cash flow disruption. Leadership distraction. Recovery costs.

This is why recovery is not just technical.

A business can restore files and still lose trust. It can recover an account and still lose customers. It can get the website back and still face legal questions. It can reopen the system and still have employees afraid to use it. It can regain control and still spend months repairing reputation.

Real recovery includes customer trust, vendor confidence, employee calm, legal documentation, financial stability, insurance coordination, regulatory obligations, clear timelines, better controls, and leadership credibility. Recovery is not only about bringing systems back online. It is about bringing the operation back under control.

Backups are central to that control, but they need to be understood correctly.

Backups are not boring. Backups are survival.

But backups are survival, not immunity.

A backup can restore files. It does not automatically restore stolen data. It does not erase exposure. It does not calm customers by itself. It does not fix legal obligations. It does not prove what happened. It does not rebuild reputation. That does not make backups less important. It means backups are one part of resilience, not the whole plan.

A backup only matters if it works. Cloud sync is not the same as backup. If ransomware encrypts files and the cloud service simply syncs the encrypted versions, the business may still be in trouble. Backups should be separated from infected systems. Recovery should be tested before disaster. Backup access must be protected. Critical documents must be recoverable. Small businesses need simple backup routines that are actually used. Backups should not be controlled by the same compromised account. Recovery time matters. Recovery proof matters.

The backup question is not, “Do I have one?” The real question is: can I restore what matters when I am under pressure?

That question should be answered before the crisis. Not during it.

Paying ransom is another area where people want a simple answer, but simple answers can be dangerous. Payment may not guarantee recovery. It may create legal, financial, or repeat-target risk. It may fund criminal activity. It may not stop stolen data from being leaked. It may not restore trust. It may not prevent the attacker from coming back. Before making any payment decision, get professional, legal, insurance, and law-enforcement guidance where appropriate.

The better message is this: do not let the ransom clock be the first time you make a plan.

Modern extortion often includes data exposure. Criminals may steal data before locking files. They may threaten to publish it, sell it, contact customers, embarrass the owner, expose private records, or damage the business. That changes the problem. If data was stolen, restoring from backup does not erase the exposure.

Now the business must ask harder questions. What was taken? Who is affected? Is regulated data involved? Are customers at risk? Are employees at risk? Are vendors at risk? Is notification required? Is legal counsel needed? Is insurance involved? Is the attacker bluffing or proving possession? What evidence exists? What can be said publicly? What should not be said yet?

This is where preparation, documentation, and calm decision-making matter. If the first time a business thinks about these questions is during the incident, the attacker already owns the clock.

Criminals use shame and pressure because pressure breaks judgment. They may say, "Pay now or we leak this." "Do not contact police." "You have 24 hours." "We will contact your clients." "We will destroy your files." "We will embarrass you." "We will keep your account." "We will post your private data." "We will ruin your business." "We will tell your customers you failed."

The goal is to isolate the victim and force fast decisions.

The response is discipline. Slow down. Preserve proof. Get help. Control communication. Do not let the attacker run the clock.

Account recovery can also become the hostage mechanism. Attackers may change recovery email addresses, recovery phone numbers, multi-factor methods, backup codes, admin accounts, domain settings, security questions, forwarding rules, connected devices, trusted sessions, OAuth apps, password manager access, or business page ownership. That means changing the password may not be enough. The attacker may still control the recovery path.

Recovery settings are critical infrastructure. Treat them that way.

Business owners should prepare before anything happens. Backups. Incident plan. Admin account inventory. Recovery contacts. Cyber insurance review. Multi-factor authentication or passkeys. Role-based access. Offboarding process. Vendor contacts. Platform recovery documents. Evidence process. Finance and payment freeze rules. Communication plan. Legal contact. Clean-device recovery plan. Domain registrar protection. Payroll emergency procedure. Customer notification draft. Employee escalation rules.

That may sound like a lot, but the goal is not to create a binder no one uses. The goal is to know who does what when control is lost. Who can make decisions? Who can contact the bank? Who can contact the domain registrar? Who can freeze payroll changes? Who can talk to customers? Who can preserve evidence? Who can approve public statements? Who can restore backups? Who can verify that a device is clean?

Without those answers, a crisis makes everyone improvise.

A strong protection system for this level of threat has to think like crisis command. It cannot only ask, "Is this suspicious?" It has to ask: what is controlled by the attacker? What is locked? What is stolen? What is threatened? What systems are still trusted? What accounts control recovery? What communication channels are clean? What data may be exposed? What business operations are blocked? What payments should be frozen? What vendors or customers are affected? What legal or insurance obligations may apply? What evidence must be preserved? What can be restored? What must stay isolated?

This is the level where everyday security becomes continuity. It is the level where prevention, response, evidence, legal readiness, vendor coordination, payroll protection, reputation protection, and system recovery have to meet in one place. A serious cybersecurity program cannot stop at alerts. It has to help leaders make decisions when the business is under pressure.

That is why the best systems are built around containment, preservation, verification, recovery, communication, and hardening. Detect control loss. Isolate affected systems. Preserve evidence. Freeze sensitive actions. Revoke sessions. Protect recovery accounts. Verify clean communication channels. Activate an incident room. Map operational impact. Notify decision-makers by role. Coordinate legal, insurance, and security response. Restore from tested recovery paths. Track reputation and customer trust. Harden against recurrence. Log every action.

This is not fear-based thinking. It is operational maturity.

The reason this matters for ordinary readers is simple: in a real hostage situation, time feels distorted. Minutes feel like seconds. Hours disappear. Everyone wants an answer immediately, but the facts are still forming. That is why the plan has to exist before the crisis. You cannot build calm after panic has already taken over the room. You build calm by deciding in advance what gets frozen, who gets called, what evidence is preserved, what accounts are protected first, and what communication channel everyone will trust.

A business should also decide what actions are automatically high risk during an incident. No vendor banking changes. No payroll changes. No new admin accounts. No public statements without review. No customer notices until facts are confirmed. No reconnecting devices because someone is impatient. No deleting messages because they are embarrassing. No paying anything because the attacker put a clock on the screen. These rules are not there to slow recovery. They are there to keep the attacker from using confusion as another weapon.

Individuals need a smaller version of the same plan. Know which email controls your most important accounts. Know how to contact your phone carrier. Know where your recovery codes are stored. Know which bank number is real. Know how to log out sessions. Know who you would call if your phone stopped working, your email locked you out, or your social media account started messaging people without you. The worst moment to search for the rescue path is after the account has already been taken.

This is also why evidence must be treated with respect. A screenshot may seem small, but it can show the timeline. A sender address may show the source. A ransom note may show what was claimed. A login alert may show when access changed. A bank notice may show how money moved. A platform email may show recovery tampering. If those pieces are deleted in the rush to clean up, the victim may lose the ability to prove what happened. Control is not only recovered through passwords and backups. Sometimes control is recovered through proof.

A digital hostage situation is not only about technology. It is about whether the person, family, business, or organization can continue functioning when someone else tries to take control. It is about whether the crisis becomes a controlled event or a collapse into panic. It is about whether the attacker controls the clock, the message, the access, and the pressure, or whether the victim has a plan strong enough to slow the attack down.

The best time to plan for a digital hostage situation is before someone else controls the keys.

This closes Part II for a reason. We have talked about cybercrime as an economy. We have talked about phishing, email, passwords, phones, and social engineering. Now we see where many of those roads can lead: loss of control. The attack may start with a message, an old password, a trusted name, a phone number, or an exposed account. But if it succeeds, the result can become a hostage situation.

Ransomware is not only about locked files. It is about control, pressure, and the fight to keep your life or business operating.

The answer is not panic. The answer is preparation.

When criminals take control, preparation is the difference between a crisis you manage and a crisis that manages you.

Part III:
The Human Side of Cybersecurity

Chapter 13

The Human Mistake Attackers Count On

Most people do not get attacked because they are stupid.

They get attacked because they are human.

They are busy. They are tired. They are helpful. They are distracted. They are hopeful. They are afraid. They are overwhelmed. They are trying to move fast. They are trying to do the right thing. They are trying to answer the customer, support the boss, protect the family, finish payroll, make the deadline, and keep life moving.

Attackers know this.

They do not need someone to be careless every day. They only need one rushed moment.

That one idea should change the way we talk about cybersecurity. Too often, when something goes wrong, the first question people ask is, "How could they fall for that?" That question may feel natural, but it is usually the wrong starting point. It turns a security failure into a character judgment. It makes people defensive. It makes victims quiet. It makes employees hide mistakes. It makes leaders believe the answer is blame instead of better design.

A mistake is not the same as stupidity.

A person can be intelligent and still click while exhausted. A person can be careful and still trust the wrong message during a stressful moment. A business owner can be responsible and still miss a fake vendor change while juggling payroll, customers, operations, and personal life. An employee can be well trained and still respond too quickly when a message appears to come from leadership.

Cybersecurity should not be built around shame. It should be built around protection.

That is the turn we are making in this part of the book. Up to this point, we have looked at the connected world, the attack surface, the business model of cybercrime, phishing, email, passwords, phones, social engineering, ransomware, account takeovers, and digital hostage situations. Now we have to look at the human being standing in the middle of all of it.

Because the human being is where many attacks succeed.

That statement is not an accusation. It is a reality. Criminals design attacks around real human behavior, not perfect behavior. They know people get tired. They know people multitask. They know people trust familiar names. They know people want to help. They know people are distracted. They know people are overconfident. They know people assume the request is normal. They know people do not want to disappoint someone. They know people believe they can spot danger in time.

They also know that most people are not operating inside a clean, quiet, controlled environment when the message arrives.

A person may be checking email between meetings. A business owner may be approving invoices from a phone while walking into an appointment. A parent may be responding to a school message while cooking dinner. An employee may be clearing a crowded inbox at the end of a long day. A bookkeeper may be handling payroll while also answering vendor questions. A founder may be reading an investor message while under financial pressure. A receptionist may be answering calls while customers are standing in front of them.

That is real life. That is the environment criminals attack.

The biggest mistake people make in cybersecurity is not always clicking the wrong link. The biggest mistake is assuming they are safe because nothing bad has happened yet. That belief leads to everything else. Clicking too fast. Trusting too quickly. Reusing passwords. Ignoring updates. Sharing too much. Not verifying. Waiting until something goes wrong. Thinking security is someone else's job. Assuming they would recognize a scam. Assuming the bank, platform, or provider will catch everything.

Security does not fail only when someone clicks. It often fails long before that, when there are no guardrails in place.

That matters because one human moment should not be able to collapse a life or business. A rushed employee should not be able to move money to a criminal without a second step. A confused parent should not have to decide alone whether a message from a child is real. A tired owner should not have every critical account tied to one phone, one email, and one reused password. A new employee should not be expected to recognize every scam without training, process, and permission to slow down.

Attackers do not need you to be careless every day. They only need you to be rushed once.

That rushed moment can become a clicked link, a shared code, a changed payment detail, a fake login, a malicious attachment, or a hidden mistake that gives the attacker time to move deeper. The damage often begins small. One code. One click. One approval. One attachment. One payment change. One conversation that should have been verified another way.

Then the chain reaction begins.

An ordinary person creates risk every day without meaning to. They click delivery links. Save passwords in browsers. Use public Wi-Fi without caution. Use one password everywhere. Share family details online. Post travel in real time. Respond to fake support messages. Give apps too much access. Ignore account alerts. Use old devices. Leave accounts logged in. Keep sensitive documents in email. Trust links from text messages. Approve login prompts without reading them.

Most of these things feel normal. That is why they are dangerous.

The average person is not waking up and deciding to be careless. They are making convenience choices inside a world that rewards speed. The fastest link is the one in the message. The easiest password is the one they already know. The simplest place to store a document is email. The easiest thing to do with an update prompt is delay it. The fastest way to approve a login is to tap yes. The easiest way to help a coworker is to send the file now and ask questions later.

Convenience feels harmless until it becomes the attacker's shortcut.

Business owners face the same problem with higher stakes. They create risk because they are carrying too much alone. No access review. Shared passwords. Former employees still active. No vendor verification. No backup testing. Too many disconnected tools. Personal email used for business. The owner controlling everything through one phone. No written incident plan. No employee training. No finance approval process. No payroll change verification. No clear reporting path. No admin account inventory.

For small businesses, the issue is often not laziness. It is overload.

The owner is trying to do five jobs at once, and security becomes one more thing on the list. The problem is that criminals do not care how overloaded the owner is. In fact, overload is useful to them. Overloaded people skip steps. Overloaded people trust familiar names. Overloaded people delay security decisions because everything else feels urgent. Overloaded people build businesses on systems that worked yesterday, even if they are no longer safe today.

Employees can also create business risk when systems rely only on them noticing danger. They approve urgent requests. Click links. Open attachments. Share codes. Use personal devices. Reuse passwords. Trust a fake boss message. Ignore suspicious emails. Avoid reporting because they are embarrassed. Send documents through the wrong channel. Accept vendor changes without verification. Leave accounts active on old devices.

The answer is not to scare employees into silence. The answer is to make reporting safe and verification normal.

Shame is one of the most dangerous forces after a cyber mistake. When people feel ashamed, they may hide the incident, delay reporting, delete evidence, try to fix it alone, keep clicking, avoid telling leadership, fail to warn coworkers, and let the attacker stay longer. Shame turns a small mistake into a bigger incident because it gives the criminal more time.

Attackers benefit from silence.

A strong security culture has to say the opposite: I would rather you ask twice than hide once.

That sentence should be posted inside every business that handles money, customers, payroll, vendors, employee data, or sensitive information. It should be repeated by owners and managers until people believe it. A person who reports quickly is not creating a problem. They are helping contain one. A person who asks whether a payment change is real is not slowing the company down. They are protecting it. A person who says, "I clicked something and I am not sure if it was safe," should be treated as someone who gave the business a chance to respond.

Leaders set the tone. If leadership reacts with anger, people hide. If leadership humiliates employees, people wait. If leadership acts like every mistake is a personal failure, people learn to protect themselves instead of the organization. But if leadership creates no-shame reporting, trains people clearly, makes verification normal, rewards escalation, documents processes, uses approval rules, gives people permission to slow down, and makes security part of operations, the business becomes harder to exploit.

A leader's job is not to pretend people will never make mistakes. A leader's job is to make sure one mistake does not become a disaster.

This is where convenience has to be understood as a tradeoff. Convenience is not evil. Convenience is why modern technology works. But convenience without control creates predictable failure. Staying logged in is convenient. Easy passwords are convenient. Shared accounts are convenient. Skipping multi-factor authentication is convenient. Clicking the fastest link is convenient. Using one device for everything is convenient. Saving sensitive files in email is convenient. Approving prompts without reading them is convenient. Avoiding updates is convenient.

Criminals do not need to invent a brand-new weakness if convenience already created one.

Being busy creates tunnel vision. People click while walking into meetings. They respond from phones. They approve requests while traveling. They handle payroll between calls. They clear inboxes too quickly. They answer customers while distracted. They click delivery links because they are expecting a package. They respond to fake legal notices because they do not have time to slow down. They approve a familiar-looking request because the day is already full.

Attackers design scams to look like normal tasks because normal tasks move fast.

They use urgency, fear, authority, helpfulness, opportunity, curiosity, routine, trust, confusion, shame, and timing. They do not need to outsmart a person at their best. They target the person when they are moving fast, distracted, or emotionally activated. They know that a person under pressure is less likely to verify. They know that a person trying to be helpful may give away information. They know that a person afraid of consequences may click before thinking. They know that a person who believes they are too smart to be fooled may skip the very steps that would protect them.

Overconfidence is dangerous because it lowers verification.

People say, "I would never fall for that." "I can spot scams." "I know what I am doing." "I am careful." "My employees know better." "My bank will catch it." "My phone is secure." "My email is fine." "That would never happen to us."

That confidence can feel like strength, but in cybersecurity it can become a blind spot. The safest people are not the ones who think they are impossible to fool. The safest people are the ones who verify anyway.

Verification is not a sign that you are weak. It is a sign that you understand the environment you are operating in. You can be smart and still verify. You can be experienced and still verify. You can trust someone and still verify a high-risk request through a known channel. Verification is not an insult to trust. Verification is how trust survives contact with a world full of impersonation.

This is why cybersecurity should be designed for human reality, not perfect behavior.

People will click. People will rush. People will forget. People will trust. People will get tired. People will make mistakes. A serious system accepts that reality and builds guardrails around it. The goal is not to eliminate every human mistake. The goal is to prevent one human mistake from becoming a disaster.

Individuals need guardrails. A password manager. Multi-factor authentication or passkeys. Account alerts. Privacy settings. App permission reviews. Unique passwords. Known-channel verification. Secure recovery codes. Device locks. Regular updates. Backup email and phone review. Session review. Phone carrier protection. Secure cloud storage for sensitive documents. These are not luxury controls. They are the digital equivalent of seatbelts, locks, and smoke detectors.

They protect people when attention fails.

Businesses need operational guardrails. Payment approval rules. Vendor change verification. Role-based access. Multi-factor authentication for critical accounts.

Offboarding checklists. Backups. Incident plans. Employee reporting workflows. Admin account reviews. Finance and payroll controls. Evidence preservation. Known-channel verification. No shared passwords for critical systems. Clean recovery contacts. Secure document storage. Customer communication plans.

These guardrails should not live only in a policy document no one reads. They should be built into the way the business operates. If vendor banking changes require independent verification, then the bookkeeper is not being difficult by slowing down. They are following the rule. If payroll changes require a second approval, then the employee is not being suspicious. They are protecting the company. If suspicious messages are reported without shame, then the team learns that escalation is part of professionalism.

Security becomes stronger when the safe action is easier than the risky action.

Consider a simple business example. An employee is rushing between tasks when a message appears to come from the owner. The message says a vendor payment is urgent and needs to be handled before the end of the day. The tone sounds normal. The request feels important. The employee does not want to delay the owner or look careless. So they approve the payment change.

Later, the business learns the message was fake.

The employee did not fail because they were stupid. The business failed because one rushed employee had the power to move money without a verification guardrail.

That is the lesson.

If the process allows one person under pressure to make an irreversible decision, the process is weak. If one email can change where money goes, the process is weak. If one phone call can extract sensitive information, the process is weak. If one fake authority claim can bypass approval rules, the process is weak. If one embarrassed employee can hide a mistake for hours or days, the culture is weak.

The answer is not to blame the person. The answer is to strengthen the process.

The same lesson applies at home. A parent receives a message that appears to come from a school, a child, a bank, or a delivery service. They are distracted. They are worried. They click. Maybe the message was fake. The answer is not shame. The answer is to know what to do next. Stop. Do not hide it. Preserve evidence. Report it if needed. Change passwords from a safe device if needed. Revoke sessions. Contact the bank or platform if needed. Tell the right person if the issue is business-related. Document what happened. Watch for follow-up attacks.

Fast reporting can be the difference between a contained incident and a spreading one.

That is why every person and every business should know the immediate response to a mistake: stop, preserve, report, contain, recover, and learn. Stop before taking more action. Preserve the message, screenshot, link, sender information, or call details. Report it to the right person or platform. Contain the damage by changing passwords from a clean device, revoking sessions, freezing payments, or contacting the bank. Recover accounts and settings carefully. Then learn what guardrail would prevent the same mistake next time.

Do not delete messages until evidence is captured. Do not try to fix everything alone. Do not let shame slow reporting. Do not assume silence makes the situation better. Silence gives attackers time.

A mature security program should treat human error as a predictable risk condition, not a moral failure. It should ask what happened around the person. Was urgency used? Was authority used? Was fear used? Was helpfulness exploited? Was the person rushed, tired, or distracted? Did the system allow one person to approve too much? Was there a missing verification step? Was there a missing access control? Was there a missing reporting path? Was shame likely to delay reporting? Was evidence preserved? Could this mistake have been prevented by a guardrail?

Those questions are more useful than asking, "Who messed up?"

The goal is to contain the damage, preserve evidence, guide recovery, and recommend the guardrail that prevents the same mistake next time. That is how an organization learns. Not through humiliation. Through improvement.

This chapter needs to be compassionate, but it also needs to be firm. Human nature is not an excuse to ignore security. It is the reason security must be designed better. Being busy is not a defense. It is a risk condition. Being helpful is not a flaw. It is something attackers exploit. Trust is not bad. It needs verification. Convenience is not evil. It needs boundaries.

You are human. That is not a defect. But criminals know how to exploit human moments, so we build habits, processes, and systems that protect you when you are not at your best.

This is the mindset shift. The goal is not to become a perfect person who never makes mistakes. The goal is to build habits, systems, and guardrails strong enough that one human moment does not become a disaster.

That means individuals protect the accounts that matter. Businesses protect the processes that matter. Leaders protect the people who report. Families talk about scams without shame. Employees get permission to slow down. Everyone learns that verification is not paranoia. It is protection.

Attackers count on the human mistake. They count on speed. They count on shame. They count on convenience. They count on fear. They count on the employee who does not want to ask twice, the owner who does not have time, the parent who panics, the customer service person who wants to help, and the founder who wants opportunity to be real.

We cannot remove humanity from cybersecurity, and we should not try. We should build security that respects human reality.

Cybersecurity fails when we expect humans to be perfect. It improves when we build systems that protect people on their worst day, not just their best one.

Chapter 14

Why Smart People Still Get Fooled

Being smart does not make you immune to scams.

That is one of the hardest truths for capable people to accept. Intelligence helps. Experience helps. Education helps. Success helps. But none of those things make a person untouchable. A scam does not always win because someone lacks intelligence. A scam wins because it reaches a human being at the right moment, with the right pressure, inside the right situation.

Smart people still get tired. Smart people still hope. Smart people still trust. Smart people still rush. Smart people still want opportunity. Smart people still want to solve problems quickly. Smart people still want to believe that the good news in front of them is real, or that the urgent problem in front of them can be fixed before it gets worse.

The scam is not built for who you are at your best. It is built for the moment when you are tired, rushed, hopeful, afraid, distracted, or trying to solve a problem quickly.

That is why the phrase, "I am too smart to fall for that," is dangerous. It sounds confident, but confidence is not a control. In some situations, that belief is exactly what scammers count on. When a person believes they are too sharp to be manipulated, they may skip the very verification steps that would have protected them.

A scam does not need you to be foolish. It needs you to be certain too soon.

That certainty can come from many places. It can come from a professional website. It can come from paperwork that looks official. It can come from a person who speaks with confidence. It can come from legal language. It can come from a familiar logo, a realistic email thread, a believable domain name, a polished proposal, a fake support person, or a process that looks organized enough to feel legitimate.

This is where capable people can be especially vulnerable. Smart people often look for structure. They look for documents. They look for a website. They look for references. They look for steps. They look for a process that appears to confirm the opportunity or the warning in front of them.

Scammers know that, so they create structure.

They may use complex documents, professional language, legal wording, investment details, fake due diligence, fake verification steps, fake references, fake contracts, fake dashboards, fake email threads, fake business registrations, fake reviews, fake support staff, fake timelines, and fake urgency wrapped in professional process. The target thinks, "This looks legitimate." But a scam can be organized. A scam can have paperwork. A scam can have a process. A scam can have a website.

The presence of structure does not prove truth.

That is the danger of verification theater. Verification theater is when a scam gives enough signs of legitimacy to make doubt feel unreasonable. It may include a professional website, legal forms, realistic emails, fake staff, fake contracts, fake reviews, fake credentials, fake names, fake business records, or a step-by-step process. The victim feels like they did their homework. But they were only verifying inside the scammer's stage.

That phrase matters: inside the scammer's stage.

A stage can look convincing while still being fake. A fake business can have a website. A fake investor can have paperwork. A fake recruiter can have a job description. A fake legal threat can have formal language. A fake vendor can have an invoice. A fake brand deal can have a contract. A fake opportunity can have a timeline. A fake support team can answer the phone. A fake dashboard can display information that appears official.

If every piece of proof comes from the same environment controlled by the requester, you have not verified independently. You have only examined the props.

Verification must happen outside the system the scammer controls.

This is one of the most important rules in the entire book. Do not verify a suspicious request using the phone number inside the message. Do not trust the website link provided by the person asking you to act. Do not rely only on paperwork sent by the person who benefits from your belief. Do not let the scammer build the question, provide the evidence, and control the path you use to confirm the answer.

The smarter the scam looks, the more independent the verification needs to be.

Smart, educated, successful, capable people get fooled because scams do not only attack knowledge. They attack timing, emotion, trust, authority, pressure, and process. A smart person can still be fooled when the timing feels believable, the opportunity feels real, the authority feels legitimate, the fear feels urgent, the request fits their world, the scam includes enough detail, the paperwork looks professional, or the person believes they already checked enough.

A scam does not need to defeat intelligence. It only needs to bypass it long enough for action.

Hope is one of the ways that happens. Hope is powerful because it pulls people toward possibility. It tells the founder that the funding may finally be here. It tells the job seeker that the right opportunity finally arrived. It tells the creator that the brand deal is real. It tells the business owner that the partnership could change everything. It tells the person who feels lonely that the relationship may be genuine. It tells the person under pressure that the solution has finally appeared.

Hope is not weakness. Hope builds businesses, careers, families, art, communities, and futures. But hope can also make people want something to be real so badly that weak proof starts to feel stronger than it is.

Scammers understand this. They use investment opportunities, business funding, new jobs, romance, partnerships, public-speaking opportunities, legal settlements, refunds, grants, emergency solutions, brand deals, and the feeling that someone finally understands your vision. That last one is especially dangerous for founders and creators. When you have been fighting for a vision, and someone appears to understand it, the relief can lower your guard.

That does not mean you should stop hoping. It means hope needs verification.

Fear works in the opposite direction, but it leads to the same risk. Fear makes people move fast. Scammers use messages like: your account will close, your bank account is locked, legal action is pending, payroll failed, there is a tax problem, your child or family member is in trouble, you are being sued, a customer is angry, you will be publicly embarrassed, you will lose access, or you missed a deadline.

Fear narrows attention. It makes people focus on stopping the threat instead of verifying whether the threat is real. A frightened person wants relief. The scammer offers relief through action: click this, pay this, confirm this, send this, log in here, do not tell anyone, act now.

Fear turns a capable person into a rushed person. A rushed person becomes easier to steer.

Authority adds another layer. People are trained to respond to authority. A bank, government agency, attorney, police officer, boss, investor, payroll provider, school, healthcare provider, platform support team, insurance company, vendor, client, or tax office can all create a feeling that the message is too important to ignore.

The more official it sounds, the more careful you should become. Authority should trigger verification, not blind obedience.

That may feel backwards at first. We are used to treating authority as a reason to move faster. But in the age of exposure, authority can be borrowed. A criminal does not need to become the bank if they can look like the bank long enough for you to click. They do not need to be the attorney if they can make a document sound legal enough to scare you. They do not need to be the boss if they can use the boss's name, tone, or compromised email account.

Success creates risk too. Successful people are not safer because they are successful. In many ways, success creates a larger attack surface. Founders, executives, creators, business owners, professionals, and public figures may have authority, visibility, reputation, audience, money movement, business contacts, decision power, admin access, vendor relationships, payroll control, brand value, and trust from others.

The more people trust your name, the more valuable your name becomes to criminals.

If a creator has an audience, a fake brand deal can be used to steal access or reputation. If an executive has authority, a fake request from that executive can move employees. If a founder is seeking capital, a fake investor process can exploit hope and pressure. If a real estate professional handles closing information, a fake wire instruction can fit the normal rhythm of the work. If a doctor or clinic handles insurance requests, a fake administrative message can look routine. If a lawyer receives legal documents all day, a malicious attachment can hide inside the job itself.

The scam adapts to the life of the target.

That is why smart-person scams often do not look like the scams people warn about in casual conversation. A founder may be fooled by a fake investor process because the documents look serious, the language sounds professional, and the opportunity matches what they need. An executive may approve a fake vendor payment because the request appears inside a normal business workflow. A lawyer may open a fake legal document because legal documents are part of the job. A clinic may respond to fake insurance requests because the request sounds administrative and urgent. A creator may respond to a fake brand deal because the offer looks polished and aligned with the audience. A parent may respond to a fake child emergency because fear outruns verification.

These are not examples of unintelligent people. They are examples of scams designed to hit the right pressure point.

That distinction matters. Victims are not proof that someone is unintelligent. Victims are proof that the scam was designed to reach the right human moment. When people believe only careless people get scammed, they stop preparing. When they understand that scams target human pressure, they build better systems.

Being busy makes capable people even easier to fool. Executives approve from phones. Owners answer messages between meetings. Parents multitask. Employees clear inboxes under pressure. Founders respond to opportunities while exhausted. Bookkeepers handle invoices while juggling deadlines. Creators respond to brand deals from direct messages. Professionals open documents because documents are part of their work.

A scam that would look obvious on a quiet day may work on a chaotic one.

Busy is not an excuse, but it is a risk condition. When people are busy, they make faster decisions with less context. They trust what looks normal because they do not have time to examine it. They treat delay as failure. They assume the process around them will catch anything serious. They believe they can clean up the details later.

Criminals understand that. They time pressure around normal workflow. They send fake invoices near payment deadlines. They send fake delivery messages when people are expecting packages. They send fake legal notices with deadlines. They send fake payroll messages near pay periods. They send fake job offers to people actively looking. They send fake investment messages to founders looking for capital. They send fake support messages when platforms are already part of daily life.

The message feels believable because it fits the moment.

Artificial intelligence makes this problem worse because it gives scammers better camouflage. It can create better writing, better research, fake credentials, fake voices, fake profiles, fake websites, fake documents, fake contracts, fake reviews, fake due-diligence materials, personalized timing, professional tone, industry-specific language, realistic customer support chats, and fake executive messages.

AI removes many of the old warning signs. The scam may no longer sound awkward. The fake document may look polished. The fake website may appear professional. The fake profile may include a believable history. The fake voice may sound familiar. The fake opportunity may be tailored to the target's goals.

That means smart people cannot rely on instinct alone.

Instinct is useful, but it is not enough. A scam can be built to feel right. It can be built to match your expectations. It can be built to arrive when the opportunity, fear, or task already makes sense. The more personalized the scam becomes, the less useful old assumptions become.

This is where pride and embarrassment make things worse. Smart people do not like admitting they were fooled. Leaders especially do not like it. They think, "I should have known better." "I do not want my team to know." "I do not want my family to think I was careless." "I do not want clients to lose trust." "I will fix it myself first." "I am the leader, so I cannot admit this happened." "I am the expert, so this is embarrassing."

That delay gives attackers time.

Shame protects the criminal. Reporting protects everyone.

The faster a mistake is reported, the faster damage can be contained. The faster a suspicious request is escalated, the more likely it can be stopped before money moves. The faster a compromised account is identified, the faster sessions can be revoked and recovery paths secured. Pride feels protective in the moment, but it often protects the wrong thing. It protects ego while the attacker moves.

Smart people should do something different. They should stop trusting instinct alone. They should verify outside the message. Slow down under pressure. Ask someone else to review high-risk decisions. Use approval rules. Separate hope from proof. Document verification. Never let urgency replace process. Treat authority as something to verify. Confirm payment changes through known channels. Use strong account protections. Build systems that force second review.

The smarter the person, the more disciplined the process should be.

That sentence may challenge some readers, and it should. Capable people sometimes believe process is for less experienced people. They believe their judgment is enough. But high-value decisions deserve more than judgment. Money movement deserves verification. Vendor changes deserve verification. Legal threats deserve escalation. Access grants deserve approval. Public statements during a crisis deserve review. Opportunities that ask for money, identity, access, or secrecy deserve independent proof.

No one is above verification.

Leaders need to teach that clearly. Owners and executives must follow the same rules as employees. High-value decisions need second review. Urgency does not override payment controls. Confidence is not a control. Reporting is strength, not embarrassment. Payment changes require known-channel verification. Legal threats require escalation. Codes are never shared. Authority does not bypass process. Smart people still need guardrails.

The strongest teams do not rely on ego. They rely on process.

This matters because authority can become a vulnerability. If everyone in the company believes the owner can bypass every rule, then anyone who impersonates the owner can try to bypass every rule too. If executives are allowed to move money without verification, a fake executive message becomes more dangerous. If leadership treats process as something only employees must follow, the business creates a gap exactly where criminals want one: at the top, near authority.

A serious security culture says that controls apply most strongly where power is greatest. The account that can approve money gets more protection. The person who can change payroll gets more verification. The executive who can pressure employees gets more process, not less. The public figure whose name people trust gets more impersonation protection. The founder whose opportunity pipeline involves investors and partners gets more independent review.

That is not disrespect. That is maturity.

For individuals, the same principle applies. If an opportunity seems perfectly aligned with what you want, verify it more carefully. If a message creates fear, slow down. If a person claims authority, confirm through a known channel. If a document looks official, verify the source outside the document. If a website looks polished, check who controls it. If a person tells you not to discuss the situation with anyone else, consider that a major warning sign.

Confidence is not verification.

A professional website is not verification. A polished document is not verification. A familiar logo is not verification. A clean email is not verification. A person who sounds calm is not verification. A process that looks official is not verification. Verification is confirmation through a source the requester does not control.

That is the rule. The smarter the scam looks, the more independent the verification needs to be.

This chapter should not make the reader feel stupid. It should make the reader feel responsible. There is a difference. Responsibility means understanding that scams are designed to bypass intelligence and attack trust, timing, emotion, and process. Responsibility means building systems that do not depend on ego. Responsibility means accepting that every person, no matter how smart, needs guardrails.

Smart people get fooled. Not because they are stupid. Because scams are not designed for stupidity. They are designed for human moments: the moment you are tired, the moment you are hopeful, the moment you are afraid, the moment you are rushed, the moment the opportunity looks like exactly what you needed, the moment the website looks professional, the moment the paperwork looks complete, the moment the person sounds official, the moment you think, "I checked enough."

That is where the scam lives.

And sometimes intelligence makes it worse, because smart people can convince themselves they did enough due diligence when all they really did was verify the stage the scammer built for them.

So no, intelligence is not enough. Confidence is not enough. A professional website is not enough. A polished document is not enough. The defense is not ego. The defense is verification.

Intelligence helps, but it is not a firewall. Verification is.

Chapter 15

Social Media, Public Records, and the Death of Privacy

Most people are not private.

They are searchable.

That may sound blunt, but it is the reality of the world we live in now. Privacy did not disappear in one dramatic moment. It was not taken all at once by one company, one platform, one government database, or one cybercriminal. Privacy leaked slowly. It was traded away through posts, apps, public records, business filings, photos, location sharing, loyalty programs, smart devices, social logins, data brokers, free tools, and the habit of sharing before thinking.

One post may not feel dangerous. One app permission may not feel dangerous. One business filing may not feel dangerous. One old address may not feel dangerous. One photo from an event may not feel dangerous. But together, those pieces can create a searchable profile of a person, family, founder, employee, public speaker, creator, or business.

Privacy does not usually die in one dramatic moment. It leaks.

And once you are searchable, you are easier to study, impersonate, manipulate, locate, pressure, and attack.

That is why privacy belongs in a cybersecurity book. Too many people still treat privacy as a personal preference, as if it only matters to people who are secretive or paranoid. That is outdated. Privacy is not only about hiding. Privacy is about controlling what strangers can learn, copy, combine, and use against you. It is about reducing the amount of raw material available to people who want to impersonate you, scam you, target your family, clone your business, or pressure you at the wrong moment.

The goal is not to disappear. For many people, disappearing is not possible and not desirable. Business owners need visibility. Public speakers need visibility. Founders need visibility. Creators need visibility. Executives need visibility. Local businesses need customers to find them. Professionals need credibility. Families need to live normal lives.

The goal is not silence. The goal is control.

Visibility and exposure are not the same thing. Visibility helps people know who you are. Exposure gives strangers unnecessary details they can use against you. A founder may need visibility. A speaker may need visibility. A creator may need visibility. A business owner may need visibility. But visibility should be intentional. Exposure is accidental.

Strategic visibility says, "Here is my mission, my work, my message, my company, and the way to reach me through the right channels." Exposure says, "Here is my hotel, my family routine, my internal dashboard, my payment workflow, my employee conflict, my vendor list, my travel schedule, and enough personal detail to build a convincing lie."

Social media became one of the playgrounds where cybercrime could grow because it made trust visible. It made identities visible. It made relationships visible. It made businesses visible. It made emotions visible. It made public timing visible. It gave criminals a massive public research tool. Social media did not create cybercrime, but it gave criminals a way to study people at scale.

People reveal far more than they think. Family members. Children. Birthdays. Travel plans. Events. Workplace. Job title. Location. Friends. Vendors. New jobs. New clients. Home details. Cars. Schools. Pets. Hobbies. Political views. Emotional struggles. Business goals. Financial stress. Celebrations. Complaints. Medical clues. Relationship status. Daily routines. Favorite places.

Each piece may feel harmless. Together, they become a research file.

A criminal can use social media to learn who you trust, where you work, who your family is, when you travel, what you care about, what you fear, what you want, what business you run, who your customers are, what vendors you use, what opportunities you are looking for, and what problems you are facing. Then they can use that information to make a scam feel personal.

A fake message works better when it sounds like it belongs in your life.

If a criminal knows you are traveling for an event, a fake hotel message may feel normal. If they know you just started a new job, a fake HR form may feel normal. If they know you are waiting on a delivery, a fake shipping message may feel normal. If they know you are seeking investors, a fake funding opportunity may feel normal. If they know your vendor relationships, a fake invoice may feel normal.

That is the danger. The scam feels personal because it was built from your own public life.

This does not mean people should never post, celebrate, speak, build a brand, or use social media. That is not realistic. The internet is part of modern life and modern business. The answer is not to vanish. The answer is to become more strategic.

Public-facing people should not disappear. They should become strategically visible. Show the mission, not every private detail. Show the brand, not every family pattern. Show the event, not the hotel in real time. Show the work, not the internal dashboard. Show leadership, not payment workflows. Show presence, not vulnerability.

If your name has value, your visibility needs a strategy.

One of the simplest privacy habits is delay. Post later, not live. Real-time posting gives people timing. It tells them where you are, where you are not, when you are distracted, and sometimes who is with you. A public speaker posting from a venue may reveal travel patterns. A family posting from an airport may reveal an empty home. A business owner posting from a conference may reveal when leadership is away.

Delay is protection.

People should be careful with high-risk information in real time: travel, hotel locations, airport photos, children's schools, home layouts, license plates, badges, screenshots, receipts, payroll details, invoice details, private documents, customer names, employee problems, legal disputes, security issues, medical documents, access cards, office entry points, and live location during events.

Again, the rule is not "never share." The rule is "think before you give strangers operational details."

Photos deserve special attention because photos often reveal more than the person intended. A photo is not just an image. It can be evidence, location data, relationship data, and operational detail. The background may show a computer screen, a badge, mail, an address, a reflection, a document, another person's face, a uniform, a school name, an office layout, a license plate, a whiteboard, a shipping label, a receipt, a hotel room, a child's routine, or a security system.

People often look at the subject of a photo. Criminals look at the edges. They look behind you. They look at the desk. They look at the screen in the background. They look at the badge around your neck, the envelope on the counter, the building sign, the whiteboard, the name tag, the license plate, and the reflection in the window.

A photo that feels harmless can reveal what a caption never says.

Oversharing also connects directly to identity theft. Criminals do not always need one perfect file. They build the file from pieces. Details like pets, schools, relatives, birthdays, hometowns, addresses, past jobs, favorite places, family names, and relationship patterns may help someone answer security questions, impersonate family members, reset accounts, open fake accounts, pass verification checks, or convince an institution they are legitimate.

Many identity attacks are built from innocent details.

A pet name may become a password clue. A school name may answer a recovery question. A birthday may help pass a verification check. A family post may help a criminal pretend to be a relative. A travel photo may help time a scam. A public complaint may reveal a company you use. A celebration may reveal a new job, new client, or new financial position.

Individually, those details look like life. Combined, they become leverage.

Business oversharing creates its own set of risks. It can support fake vendor messages, fake customer complaints, fake executive requests, fake job offers, fake brand deals, fake investment opportunities, fake business pages, fake support accounts, fake invoices, fake legal notices, fake payroll requests, and fake partnership outreach. The more criminals know about how a business operates, the easier it is to imitate normal.

That is one of the most important sentences in this chapter: the more criminals know about how you operate, the easier it is to imitate normal.

A business that publicly shows its dashboards, payment tools, vendors, internal problems, staff structure, office routines, customer details, or support workflows may be giving criminals the language they need to fool someone. A fake customer complaint sounds stronger when it uses real product details. A fake vendor request sounds stronger when the vendor relationship is public. A fake executive message sounds stronger when leadership style is visible.

Visibility builds business. Exposure gives criminals material.

Public records add another layer. Public records matter because they can expose real-world identity and business structure. Business registrations, corporate filings, court records, property records, licensing records, professional registrations, charity or nonprofit filings, political donations, domain registrations, government databases, registered agents, business addresses, and ownership details can all reveal information that feels administrative but becomes useful to a criminal.

Public does not always mean harmless.

A small business owner may not realize how much can be learned from a filing. Owner name. Business address. Registered agent. Company structure. Licensing. Industry. Related entities. Sometimes domain information or professional records. A criminal can use that information to impersonate the business, target the owner, contact employees, create fake vendor messages, build fake invoices, or clone the business online.

Small businesses need visibility, but they also need exposure control.

Data brokers and people-search sites make this problem harder. This is not about turning the conversation into a conspiracy. It is practical. Data brokers collect, package, sell, combine, reuse, and sometimes expose personal information. One site may show an address. Another may show relatives. Another may show phone numbers. Another may show business links. Another may show old locations. Together, that becomes a map.

These sites may expose addresses, phone numbers, emails, relatives, age, possible associates, property information, past locations, employment clues, social profiles, business links, court or public-record references, household members, and neighborhood information. For public-facing people, founders, creators, executives, and families, this can become a safety issue, not just a privacy annoyance.

People should search themselves. Remove what they can. Use opt-out tools where possible. Limit future exposure. Separate personal and business contact information. Use a business address where appropriate. Review privacy settings.

Repeat regularly because data can return. Monitor for impersonation. Avoid posting information that helps refill broker profiles. Protect family members where possible.

Privacy is not one cleanup. It is maintenance.

Convenience is another reason privacy keeps disappearing. Convenience often trades privacy for speed. Social logins. Apps asking for contacts. Apps asking for location. Apps asking for photo access. Staying logged in. Allowing tracking. Using one email everywhere. Syncing everything. Public wish lists. Loyalty programs. Delivery apps. Smart devices. Cloud backups. Free apps. Browser autofill. "Sign in with" shortcuts. App permissions accepted without review.

Convenience is not automatically bad. But every convenience has a data cost.

Free does not always mean harmless. Sometimes free means the service is funded by attention, advertising, tracking, behavior data, or personal information. The point is not that every free tool is evil. The point is that users should understand the trade. If you are not paying with money, you may be paying with data, attention, behavior, or exposure.

Individuals need privacy habits. Post later, not live. Limit personal details. Review app permissions. Lock down profiles. Use unique emails where useful. Remove old accounts. Separate personal and business presence. Avoid posting documents or screenshots. Think before tagging family. Search yourself regularly. Remove data broker listings where possible. Protect children's information. Review location sharing. Check photo backgrounds. Avoid using one account for everything. Limit public recovery clues.

The goal is not to become silent. The goal is to become intentional.

Business owners need privacy habits too. Limit public staff details. Protect vendor names. Avoid showing dashboards. Use professional domain emails. Protect domain records. Monitor fake pages. Control who posts as the business. Use business addresses where possible. Avoid exposing payment workflows.

Train employees on safe posting. Keep internal issues off public channels. Avoid posting client names without permission. Delay event and location posts. Protect payroll, invoice, and customer details. Monitor brand impersonation. Create official verified channels where possible.

Business privacy is part of business security.

A company that exposes too much of its workflow makes it easier for criminals to imitate that workflow. A company that exposes too many employee details makes it easier to target those employees. A company that exposes vendors, customers, invoices, or internal conflict gives outsiders more context than they need. A company that lets anyone post as the business without control risks reputation and impersonation problems.

This is why every person and business needs a privacy audit. Not a complicated audit at first. Start with questions.

What can strangers find about me? What can strangers find about my business? What can be used to impersonate me? What can be used to answer security questions? What reveals where I am or when I am away? What reveals who I trust? What reveals how my business operates? What shows my family? What shows my vendors? What shows my customers? What shows my money movement? What shows my routines? What shows my weak points?

Those questions turn privacy from an abstract concern into a practical attack-surface map.

A strong cybersecurity program should treat public exposure as a risk layer. It should not only ask whether data was stolen. It should ask what is already being given away. What is publicly searchable? What could be used for impersonation? What could be used for identity theft? What could answer security questions? What reveals physical location, travel, family members, vendors, customers, business workflows, financial pressure, emotional pressure points, or operational habits?

Some exposure is unavoidable. Licensed professionals may be listed in public databases. Business owners may need filings. Property owners may appear in records. Public speakers may have event pages. Creators may need public profiles. Executives may appear on company websites. Nonprofits may have public filings. Domains, addresses, registrations, and affiliations may not disappear just because we wish they would.

You cannot erase yourself from the internet completely, but you can reduce unnecessary exposure and control what you reveal.

That is a realistic and empowering message. Total invisibility is not the goal. Reduced unnecessary exposure is the goal. Monitored unavoidable exposure is the goal. Strategic visibility is the goal.

For public-facing people, this becomes even more important. Delay posts. Use separate public and private accounts. Control contact channels. Monitor impersonation. Limit family exposure. Use a business mailing address. Document fake profiles. Create verified official channels where possible. Avoid sharing live location. Protect travel details. Separate public brand from private life. Have a response plan. Monitor data broker exposure. Lock down account recovery.

Visibility needs a security plan.

This is especially true for people whose names carry trust. A speaker's name can be used to sell fake events. A creator's name can be used for fake brand deals. A business owner's name can be used for fake invoices. A nonprofit leader's name can be used for fake donation requests. An executive's name can be used to pressure employees. A parent's public information can be used to target a child or family member.

When your name becomes valuable, your exposure becomes valuable too.

Privacy is no longer the default. It is something you have to actively manage. Privacy settings help, but they are not a force field. Screenshots can be taken.

Friends can share posts. Platforms can change settings. Old posts can resurface. Public comments can be searched. Photos can reveal backgrounds. Connections can reveal relationships. A private account can still expose patterns.

Social media privacy is not only about who can see the post. It is about what the post reveals.

The practical answer is not fear. It is discipline. Review what is public. Reduce what does not need to be public. Separate personal and business information. Think before posting in real time. Search yourself. Search your business. Remove what can be removed. Monitor what cannot. Teach employees safe posting. Protect family members. Stop showing strangers the parts of your life and business they do not need to see.

You do not have to disappear to be safer. You have to stop giving strangers a map.

Chapter 16

The Family, Employee, and Vendor Problem

Cybersecurity is not only about you anymore.

That may be one of the most important lessons in this book. Your risk does not stop at your own phone, your own password, your own email, or your own social media account. You are also exposed through the people and systems connected to you.

Attackers do not always come straight at the person or business they want. Sometimes they come through a spouse, a child, an employee, an assistant, a vendor, a contractor, a client, a bookkeeper, a payroll provider, a social media manager, a platform, a bank, or an old account that still has access.

Modern cybersecurity is not only about blocking strangers. It is about managing trust.

That is why I call this the family, employee, and vendor problem. Not because family members, employees, and vendors are the enemy. They are not. Families need trust. Businesses need employees. Companies need vendors. Leaders need assistants. Customers need support. Communities need connection. Relationships are necessary.

But every relationship that carries access also carries risk.

You are not only exposed through your own habits. You are exposed through the people and systems connected to you. Someone connected to you may become the doorway. A family member may share too much. An employee may click a fake request. A vendor may get compromised. A contractor may keep old access. A client may send a malicious file. An assistant may receive a fake executive message. A payroll provider may become a target. A social media manager may control a public page. A former employee may still have credentials.

Attackers look for the easiest path. Sometimes the easiest path is not you. It is someone near you.

That is not a reason to stop trusting people. It is a reason to put boundaries around trust.

Family is part of the cybersecurity conversation because modern households share systems. Families share devices, Wi-Fi, streaming accounts, cloud storage, photos, passwords, phone plans, tablets, smart home devices, payment cards, school accounts, gaming accounts, email recovery, family location sharing, and social media posts. A child's account, a spouse's device, an older parent's phone, or a shared password can become a doorway into the household.

Family security is not about suspicion. It is about protection.

Criminals use family information because family creates emotion. A fake child emergency message gets attention. A grandparent scam creates panic. A fake school message feels urgent. A fake medical issue creates fear. A fake travel problem creates pressure. A spouse impersonation may lower defenses. Family details can help answer security questions. Photos can help build fake profiles. Children's names can create urgency. Family phone plans can become recovery paths. Weaker family accounts can be used to reach a stronger target.

Family details make scams feel personal. That is why oversharing matters.

Children and teenagers deserve special attention. They are growing up inside systems designed to collect attention and data. They may create risk through oversharing, gaming accounts, social media direct messages, school accounts, weak passwords, clicking links, online friendships, location sharing, family photos, using parents' devices, using parents' cards, downloading unknown apps, sharing private family details, trusting fake giveaways, or talking to strangers in games and apps.

This is not about blaming kids. Children and teenagers need guidance, not shame. They need to understand that the internet is not just entertainment. Gaming accounts can hold payment information. Social media messages can come from fake people. School portals can expose family details. A fake giveaway may be designed to steal an account. A stranger in a game may be collecting information, not just chatting.

Parents do not need to scare children into silence. They need to build habits early. Do not share family details with strangers. Do not send codes. Do not click links from unknown messages. Do not post locations without thinking. Do not use parents' cards without permission. Tell an adult if someone asks for private information, money, photos, passwords, or secrecy.

Older adults are also targeted heavily because criminals use fear, authority, loneliness, confusion, and urgency. Fake tech support calls. Fake bank calls. Romance scams. Medicare or insurance scams. Family emergency scams. Fake government notices. Gift card scams. Account takeover. Charity scams. Sweepstakes scams. Fake investment opportunities.

The damage is not only financial. Many older victims feel shame and isolation after fraud. They may be embarrassed to tell their children. They may fear losing independence. They may try to fix it alone. That silence helps criminals. Families need a no-shame plan so older relatives can report suspicious messages before money is lost.

A family security plan should feel protective, not controlling. Talk about scams. Use unique passwords. Lock devices. Protect children's privacy. Protect older relatives. Never share codes. Review family phone plans. Set emergency verification phrases. Teach children not to share family details. Use parental controls where appropriate. Separate financial accounts from casual devices.

Review location sharing. Limit real-time posting. Protect shared cloud accounts. Keep recovery contacts updated. Watch for elder fraud without shaming.

The same principle applies to businesses.

If an employee touches one computer system, they are part of the security system. That does not mean every employee must become a cybersecurity expert. It means the business must recognize that every person with access can affect the company's safety.

An employee may access email, files, payroll, customer records, CRM, invoices, social media, vendor portals, documents, calendars, or payment systems. If they can open the door, they are part of the door.

Employee risk often comes from ordinary habits, not bad intentions. Reused passwords. Personal devices. Public Wi-Fi. Clicking links. Opening attachments. Sharing codes. Approving urgent requests. Using personal email. Saving files locally. Ignoring alerts. Not reporting mistakes. Leaving devices unlocked. Taking data when they leave. Using unauthorized apps. Forwarding business files to personal accounts. Sharing logins with coworkers.

Most employee risk is not malicious. It is unmanaged.

That word matters. Unmanaged risk grows quietly. A shared password may seem convenient until no one knows who used it. A personal device may seem harmless until it becomes the only phone that can approve a company login. A former employee may seem trustworthy until their old account is used by someone else. An employee may not report a suspicious message because they fear being blamed. A staff member may approve a vendor change because the process never told them to verify another way.

Leadership can create employee risk without realizing it. No training. No clear process. No reporting path. Punishing questions. Rushing staff. No access reviews. No offboarding checklist. Shared accounts. Too many disconnected tools. No vendor verification rules. No payment approval rules. No written incident plan. No clear owner for security. No limits on who can access what.

If leaders make speed more important than verification, employees will act fast and skip controls.

A rushed culture becomes an attack surface.

This is why leadership matters. A business cannot tell employees to be careful while also punishing them for slowing down. It cannot tell employees to report suspicious messages while making them feel foolish for asking questions. It cannot demand security while giving everyone shared passwords, unclear rules, and too many disconnected tools.

A safe culture makes verification normal.

Former employees are a major part of this problem. Most businesses do not realize how much access remains after someone leaves. Old logins. Shared passwords. Email access. Cloud storage access. Social media access. CRM access. Payroll or HR access. Vendor portal access. Admin accounts. Company devices. Personal devices with company data. Browser-saved passwords. App sessions. Shared files. Group chats. Recovery emails or phone numbers.

That is dangerous.

The offboarding rule should be simple: when someone leaves, access ends before the relationship fully ends, not days or weeks later.

Offboarding should not be emotional or delayed. It should be a checklist. Disable accounts. Revoke sessions. Recover devices. Rotate shared passwords. Remove admin rights. Transfer ownership. Remove cloud access. Remove social media access. Remove payroll or HR access. Check connected apps. Document the closure.

A clean ending protects both the business and the former employee.

It protects the business because access is closed. It protects the former employee because no one can later blame them for activity that happened after they left. Access that stays open after a relationship ends creates confusion, suspicion, and risk for everyone involved.

Vendors create another major risk layer because vendors often touch important systems. They may handle payroll, IT, accounting, marketing, insurance, HR, benefits, cloud tools, legal documents, customer data, payment systems, website hosting, software updates, support tickets, and business communications. Vendors can be breached. Vendors can be impersonated. Vendors can send invoices. Vendors can request access. Vendors can become a doorway into your company.

Vendor trust needs boundaries.

Vendor-related attacks can include fake banking changes, fake invoices, compromised vendor email, fake support tickets, fake software updates, fake contractor messages, vendor portal compromise, supply-chain attacks, payment redirection, fake onboarding forms, fake renewal notices, fake insurance requests, fake tax forms, and fake contract updates.

A vendor message does not feel like an attack because vendors contact businesses all the time. That is why vendor impersonation works so well.

A business expects invoices. It expects support messages. It expects renewal notices. It expects payment updates. It expects files. It expects forms. It expects someone from payroll, insurance, accounting, marketing, IT, or software support to reach out. Criminals hide inside that routine. They make the attack look like normal business.

That is the essence of third-party risk. In plain English, third-party risk means your security can be affected by companies, contractors, platforms, and people outside your direct control. You may protect your own accounts well. But if your payroll provider, vendor, contractor, cloud platform, IT company, marketing agency, payment processor, or software provider is compromised, your business may still be affected.

Your security is connected to their security.

That does not mean you can control every vendor completely. You cannot. But you can control how much access they have, how long they have it, what they can change, how payment changes are verified, and how quickly access ends when the work ends.

Before trusting a vendor request, business owners should verify payment changes through a known channel, keep vendor contacts documented, use approval rules, limit vendor access, review vendor permissions, require multi-factor authentication where possible, remove vendor access when work ends, avoid relying only on email threads, monitor unusual invoice changes, confirm new banking details outside email, keep a vendor master record, require a second review for payment changes, and track who approved vendor changes.

Vendor requests should be trusted only after the process confirms them.

Clients and customers can also become part of the risk. Businesses want to help customers quickly, and attackers exploit that. Fake customer complaints. Malicious attachments. Chargeback fraud. Account takeover. Fake support requests. Impersonated customers. Customer data exposure. Social media complaints used as pressure. Fake refund demands. Fake legal threats. Fraudulent orders. Stolen credit cards. Fake identity documents.

A customer issue can become a security issue when it asks the business to open a file, click a link, refund money, reveal information, bypass a policy, or respond publicly under pressure.

Assistants, bookkeepers, contractors, and outside service providers deserve special attention because they often control sensitive workflows. They may access calendars, emails, invoices, cards, passwords, files, social media, customer systems, admin tools, vendor portals, payment processors, cloud drives, CRM, payroll, and legal documents.

The issue is not that these people are untrustworthy. The issue is that their access must match their role.

Helpful people should not have unlimited power by accident.

The people closest to you often need access. That does not mean they need unlimited access.

A spouse may need emergency access. A child may need device protection. An assistant may need calendar access. A bookkeeper may need invoice access. A vendor may need system access. An employee may need customer access. But each person should have only the access they need, for only as long as they need it.

That is not distrust. That is discipline.

This is the idea behind least privilege. Give people the minimum access required to do the job well. Not because you expect them to do something wrong, but because limited access limits damage if something goes wrong. If an employee account is compromised, limited access reduces what the attacker can reach. If a vendor is breached, limited access reduces what can spread. If a contractor leaves, expiring access reduces what remains behind. If a family device is compromised, separation limits what the attacker can reach.

Trust without boundaries becomes risk.

Businesses should use role-based access, least privilege, multi-factor authentication, access reviews, offboarding checklists, vendor verification, payment approval rules, device policies, employee training, no-shame reporting, vendor access expiration, separate admin accounts, audit logs, admin account reviews, vendor master records, contractor access expiration, payroll and finance controls, customer data protection, and incident reporting workflows.

This may sound like a lot, but the principle is simple: know who has access, know what they can touch, know whether they still need it, and know how to remove it quickly.

That is the kind of question every person and business should ask regularly. Who can open doors into my life or business? Who has access to email? Who has access to files? Who has access to social media? Who has access to payroll? Who has access to bank accounts? Who has access to vendor portals? Who has access to customer data? Who has access because they need it, and who has access because no one remembered to remove it?

This is not paranoia. It is mature trust management.

Consider a few ordinary examples. A former employee still has access to the business social page. Months later, the page is changed, deleted, sold, or used to message customers. A vendor email is compromised and sends a fake invoice. The business pays the criminal because the request appears to come from a trusted relationship. A teenager's gaming account exposes family payment details after a fake giveaway or malicious link. An assistant receives a fake executive request and shares a document because the message sounds urgent and confidential. A contractor still has cloud access months after the project ends and can still view files, client information, or internal documents.

These are not stranger-only attacks. They are relationship attacks.

That is why modern security has to mature beyond the idea of protecting a single user from unknown outsiders. The real world is connected. Families are connected. Businesses are connected. Vendors are connected. Customers are connected. Platforms are connected. Former employees, contractors, assistants, and outside providers may all sit somewhere near the systems that matter.

Modern security does not mean you stop trusting family, employees, vendors, or clients. It means you stop giving unlimited trust without controls.

Trust should exist. But trust should have boundaries, records, approvals, expiration dates, and recovery paths. Healthy trust is not blind. Healthy trust is managed.

A strong cybersecurity program should treat connected people and vendors as part of the risk surface. It should ask: who has access? What can they access? Do they still need it? Is the access role-based? Is multi-factor authentication enabled? Are shared passwords being used? Are former employees still active? Are vendors still connected after work ended? Are payment changes verified? Are family accounts exposing sensitive information? Are older relatives protected from scams? Are children oversharing? Are contractors using personal devices? Are assistants controlling high-risk systems? Is vendor access logged? Are customer requests being used as pressure? Is there a no-shame reporting path?

Those questions are not just technical. They are human. They recognize that security lives in relationships, not only in devices.

The answer is a trust boundary map. Know family access. Employee access. Vendor access. Contractor access. Client and customer risk. Assistant and bookkeeper access. Former employee access. Shared accounts. Admin accounts. Payment authority. Social media control. Cloud and file access. Payroll and HR access. Expired access. Missing authentication. Unverified vendor changes. High-risk trust relationships.

The map should answer one simple question: who can open doors into your life or business?

Once you know the doors, you can manage them.

You can protect the family without controlling every conversation. You can trust employees without giving everyone admin access. You can work with vendors without letting them keep permanent access. You can serve customers without opening every file they send. You can use assistants, contractors, and bookkeepers without turning helpful access into unlimited power.

That is the balance. Not fear. Not suspicion. Not isolation. Balance.

Cybersecurity is not only about protecting yourself from strangers. It is about managing the trust, access, and relationships that surround your life and business.

Trust people, but control access - because in the digital world, every relationship can become a doorway.

Chapter 17

AI, Deepfakes, and the Collapse of "Seeing Is Believing"

In the AI era, seeing is not proof.

Hearing is not proof. A polished message is not proof. A professional document is not proof. A familiar writing style is not proof. A profile photo is not proof. A voice that sounds like someone you know is not proof.

Verification is proof.

That is the trust equation now. For generations, people were taught to believe what they could see with their own eyes or hear with their own ears. A voice felt personal. A video felt convincing. A photograph felt like evidence. A document with a logo and legal language felt official. A screenshot felt like proof. A social media profile with photos, posts, and comments felt like a real person.

Artificial intelligence has changed that. It has not made truth disappear, but it has made deception more believable. It has made fake voices easier to create, fake documents easier to polish, fake profiles easier to build, fake business pages easier to imitate, and fake messages easier to personalize. It has removed many of the old warning signs people used to rely on.

That does not mean every image, voice, video, document, or message is fake. It means none of them should be treated as proof by themselves when money, identity, access, reputation, family safety, or business authority is involved.

The answer is not panic. The answer is verified trust.

A deepfake, in plain English, is fake or manipulated audio, video, image, or identity content made to look or sound real. It might be a video of a person saying something they never said. It might be a voice that sounds like a child, boss, client, spouse, vendor, executive, or public figure. It might be an image or profile used to impersonate someone who does not exist or someone who does exist but has no idea their identity is being used.

The danger is not only that the content is fake. The danger is that it can make people act as if it is real.

That is the point people misunderstand. They hear deepfake and think about celebrity videos, political clips, or funny internet tricks. That is too narrow. Deepfakes and AI-generated impersonation can become tools for scams, fraud, reputation damage, blackmail, business fraud, identity attacks, family emergency scams, fake executive approvals, fake brand endorsements, fake legal or public-relations crises, public humiliation, extortion, harassment, market manipulation, and social engineering.

Deepfakes are not just content. They are weapons against trust.

Cybersecurity has always depended on trust signals. We trust a voice because it sounds familiar. We trust a message because the tone feels right. We trust a document because it looks official. We trust a profile because it has a photo and a history. We trust a video because we think we are seeing reality. AI attacks those signals directly.

It lets a criminal create better fake emails, better fake voices, better fake videos, fake customer service, fake executives, fake recruiters, fake investors, fake romantic partners, fake legal threats, fake documents, fake screenshots, fake social profiles, fake business pages, fake reviews, fake support chats, fake contracts, and fake invoices. The scam no longer has to look sloppy. AI helps criminals remove the old warning signs.

This is why the phrase seeing is believing no longer works in the same way. Seeing may still be a signal. Hearing may still be a signal. A professional document may still be a signal. But a signal is not proof. The more important the action being requested, the more verification matters.

Voice cloning is one of the most personal examples. Voice used to feel intimate. If you heard your child, spouse, boss, client, or parent, you believed the voice because it sounded like them. Today, a voice alone cannot carry the same weight.

A fake voice can be used to create a fake call from a child, a fake executive payment approval, a fake vendor confirmation, a fake bank confirmation, a fake emergency message, a fake client instruction, a fake assistant request, a fake manager request, a fake spouse message, a fake grandparent scam, or a fake kidnapping threat. The voice may not need to be perfect. It only needs to be believable in the moment when the listener is scared, rushed, or trying to help.

That changes the rule: never send money, codes, access, or sensitive information based only on a voice.

Families are especially vulnerable because emotion moves faster than verification. A parent hearing what sounds like a child in distress may not stop to analyze the audio. A grandparent hearing what sounds like a grandchild may respond before thinking. A spouse hearing a desperate message may act quickly because love creates urgency. Criminals understand that family pressure can bypass normal caution.

AI-generated impersonation can create fake child emergencies, fake spouse or partner messages, grandparent scams, fake kidnapping threats, fake voice requests for money, fake medical emergencies, fake travel emergencies, and fake videos or images used for humiliation, extortion, or manipulation. The technology matters, but the emotional pressure matters more.

That is why families need trust anchors before the crisis.

A trust anchor is a reliable verification method agreed on before emotions take over. It might be a family emergency phrase, a known phone number, a trusted relative to call, or a rule that no one sends money based only on one call or one message. It gives people something real to hold onto when fake evidence appears.

The time to create a family emergency phrase is not during the fake emergency. The time to teach children not to panic-send information is not after someone has already impersonated them. The time to talk to older relatives about voice scams is not after money is gone. Families need simple rules that feel protective, not paranoid.

Verify emergencies through another channel. Use known numbers, not numbers provided in the message. Do not share codes. Never send money based only on a voice call. Preserve suspicious clips or messages. Teach children that secrecy and urgency are warning signs. Protect older relatives without shaming them. That is how families build verified trust.

Businesses face a different version of the same problem. Companies are built on authority and workflow. Employees are trained to respond to executives, clients, vendors, managers, payroll, legal notices, customer complaints, and urgent operational needs. AI can imitate those signals.

A fake CEO instruction can push finance to approve a payment. A fake vendor confirmation can validate a fraudulent invoice. A fake customer complaint can create panic. A fake employee message can request payroll changes. A fake brand spokesperson can damage reputation. A fake legal or public-relations crisis can force a rushed response. A fake product claim can confuse customers. A fake public statement can move faster than the company's correction.

The biggest danger is not only that the fake exists. The danger is that someone acts before the fake is verified.

No payment should be approved based only on voice, video, or email. No payroll change should be accepted because someone sounded like the right person. No vendor banking change should be confirmed by a phone number provided in the same suspicious message. No public statement should be rushed because a fake clip is spreading. No executive request should bypass process because the voice sounds familiar.

No high-risk action should be approved by appearance alone.

Businesses need known-channel verification, dual approval for finance, payroll, and vendor changes, employee training on AI scams, monitoring for fake profiles and pages, evidence preservation, crisis communication planning, documented official communication channels, executive verification rules, second review for urgent requests, and vendor contact records that live outside email threads.

This is not about slowing every part of the company. It is about adding friction where the damage can be serious. Money movement deserves friction. Payroll deserves friction. Admin access deserves friction. Public statements during a crisis deserve friction. Legal threats deserve friction. Vendor changes deserve friction. A deepfake attack is designed to create speed. A good process creates verification.

Public-facing people face an even sharper version of this threat. For public speakers, founders, creators, executives, talent, public-facing businesses, and high-profile families, identity is not only private information. Identity is an asset. A voice, face, name, audience, likeness, and public reputation can all be misused.

The more people trust your face, voice, or name, the more valuable it becomes to criminals.

A public speaker can be targeted with a fake interview or fake endorsement. A creator can be used in a fake brand deal or fake fundraising message. An executive can be used in a fake payment approval or fake public statement. A founder can be targeted with a fake investor process. A public figure can be harmed by fake scandal videos, fake voice clips, fake private messages, fake political or social statements, fake romantic messages, fake charity appeals, and fake reputation attacks.

This is why identity protection becomes more than password protection. It becomes reputation defense. It becomes evidence collection. It becomes official-channel control. It becomes legal readiness. It becomes knowing what is real before the fake spreads faster than the truth.

That is the truth behind the kind of protection public-facing people now need. It is not enough to protect an account after it is hacked. The public identity itself has to be monitored. Fake profiles have to be documented. Official channels have to be clear. Followers, clients, customers, and partners need to know where legitimate communication comes from. Legal, public-relations, and security support may need to be ready before a crisis appears.

For public-facing people, identity defense is reputation defense.

AI also makes fake profiles more believable. A fake profile can now have realistic photos, consistent bios, AI-written posts, fake histories, fake comments, fake mutual interests, fake business credentials, fake reviews, fake messages matching your tone or industry, fake engagement, fake customer support personas, fake recruiter personas, and fake brand representatives.

A fake profile can now have a backstory. That makes it harder to dismiss at a glance.

In the past, a fake account might look empty, awkward, or obviously suspicious. Now it may have enough activity to look alive. It may comment on relevant topics. It may use industry language. It may appear to know your world. It may reach out with a message that sounds like it belongs. Again, the profile does not have to be perfect. It only has to be believable long enough to start the conversation.

AI-generated documents create the same problem. Contracts, invoices, legal notices, insurance forms, tax forms, job offers, investment documents, grant documents, letters of intent, settlement notices, business proposals, vendor forms, HR documents, fake receipts, and fake screenshots can all be made to look polished quickly.

A document can look official and still be false. A logo, legal language, and professional formatting do not prove legitimacy.

That is why people need to stop treating appearance as proof. A voice by itself is not proof. A video by itself is not proof. A screenshot by itself is not proof. A profile photo by itself is not proof. A polished document by itself is not proof. A logo by itself is not proof. A professional email by itself is not proof. Caller ID by itself is not proof. A social media profile by itself is not proof. A familiar writing style by itself is not proof. A message that sounds like someone you know is not proof.

Appearance is not proof.

What should replace appearance? Verification outside the content. Known-channel verification. Pre-agreed family phrases. Second approvals. Official portals typed manually. Known phone numbers. Secure internal workflows. Documented payment rules. Video callbacks through known accounts. Evidence preservation. Independent confirmation. Verified business contacts. Secure recovery contacts. Official app communication. Role-based approval.

The rule is simple: do not verify the fake using tools the fake gave you.

If someone sends a phone number inside a suspicious message, do not use that number as proof. If a fake website gives you a support chat, do not treat that chat as independent verification. If a document contains contact information, do not assume the contact information proves the document. If a voice call asks for money, do not call back using the number the caller provides. Go outside the content. Use a known source. Use an established channel. Use a trust anchor.

Trust anchors are what let people stay calm when the fake looks real. A family emergency phrase. A verified executive callback number. An approved vendor payment-change workflow. A known legal contact. An official public-relations channel. A secure internal approval path. A verified brand-deal contact. A trusted recovery contact. An official social media channel list. These should be defined before the crisis.

When a high-risk request arrives by voice, video, email, text, social media, document, or profile, the question becomes: does this match a trust anchor? If not, slow down until independent verification happens.

If you are targeted by a deepfake or AI impersonation, the first step is not panic. The first step is preservation. Do not help the fake spread while trying to prove it is fake. Preserve evidence. Document where it appeared. Capture screenshots, links, usernames, timestamps, platform details, and the exact content if it is safe and legal to preserve. Report it to the platform. Notify trusted contacts or your team. Lock down related accounts. Issue a controlled statement if needed. Contact legal, public-relations, or security support if the matter is serious. Monitor for spread. Watch for follow-up scams. Record all actions taken.

That last piece matters. A fake clip may be only the opening move. The follow-up may be a scam message, a fake reporter inquiry, a fake legal threat, a fake support account, or a request for payment to remove the content. When someone is embarrassed or afraid, they may be easier to manipulate. Criminals know this. That is why evidence, calm, and a response plan matter.

This chapter should be serious, but not hopeless. AI has made deception more believable, but it has not made verification impossible. It has changed what counts as proof. It has raised the cost of blind trust. It has made appearance weaker and process stronger.

That is why the future belongs to people and businesses that stop treating appearance as proof. The ones that create trust anchors. The ones that verify outside the message. The ones that teach employees that a voice is not enough. The ones that teach families not to send money based only on panic. The ones that protect public identity as an asset. The ones that preserve evidence instead of reacting emotionally. The ones that build response plans before a fake spreads.

A strong protection system in the AI era should treat AI-generated impersonation as a verified-trust problem. It should ask whether the content is requesting money, access, identity, secrecy, or urgent action. It should ask whether the proof is only visual or audio. It should ask whether a known-channel verification path exists. It should ask whether the request bypasses normal approval. It should ask whether a public-facing person, executive, child, older adult, vendor, or family member is involved. It should ask whether the content is designed to create panic, shame, urgency, or reputational fear.

Most of all, it should warn against acting on appearance alone.

This is the new rule of trust. A voice can be a clue, but not the whole case. A video can be a signal, but not the verdict. A screenshot can be a starting point, but not the proof. A polished document can be reviewed, but not blindly accepted. A social profile can be inspected, but not trusted without confirmation. A familiar writing style can be noticed, but not obeyed without process.

Seeing is not believing anymore. Hearing is not believing anymore. A professional document is not believing. A polished email is not believing. A profile photo is not believing. A video is not believing. A voice that sounds like someone you love is not enough.

The danger is not only that the fake exists. The danger is that people act before they verify.

A parent hears what sounds like their child and sends money. An employee hears what sounds like the CEO and approves a payment. A founder sees what looks like an investor process and shares documents. A public figure sees a fake video spread before they can respond. A business sees a fake statement damage trust before the truth catches up.

That is why we need better rules. Not fear. Not panic. Rules. Trust anchors. Known channels. Second approvals. Evidence preservation. Crisis plans. Official communication paths. Independent confirmation.

In the AI era, trust cannot depend on what looks real. It has to depend on what can be verified.

Chapter 18

Trust, But Verify Everything

Trust is still necessary.

Families need trust. Businesses need trust. Employees need trust. Customers need trust. Vendors need trust. Public speakers need trust. Communities need trust. Without trust, life becomes impossible and business becomes unworkable.

But blind trust is dangerous now.

That is the balance this chapter has to make clear. The answer to cybercrime is not to trust no one. That is not life. That is not leadership. That is not family. That is not business. The answer is to stop using blind trust for high-risk decisions.

In the digital age, trust cannot depend only on a familiar name, a familiar voice, a logo, a polished email, a professional document, caller ID, a social media profile, or a message that sounds right. Those things may be signals, but they are not proof. A fake voice can sound real. A fake email can look professional. A fake vendor can use real details. A fake profile can look active. A fake document can look official. A fake emergency can feel urgent. A fake opportunity can feel like a breakthrough.

So the rule is simple: trust people, but verify high-risk actions.

That is not paranoia. It does not mean accusing everyone. It does not mean treating family members, employees, vendors, clients, customers, or partners like enemies. It means understanding that the threat has changed. When criminals can borrow names, clone voices, imitate brands, copy documents, spoof email, and manipulate emotion, responsible trust needs a process.

Verification is not the opposite of trust. Verification is how trust survives.

People misunderstand verification because they often hear it as an insult. They think verifying means they are being rude, suspicious, difficult, slow, or distrustful. A bookkeeper may hesitate to call a vendor back because they do not want to offend them. An employee may hesitate to question a message from the owner because they do not want to look disrespectful. A family member may hesitate to check an emergency story because they do not want to seem uncaring. A founder may hesitate to question an investor because they do not want to lose the opportunity.

That mindset has to change.

Verification is a safety habit. It is the digital version of checking both ways before crossing the street. You are not accusing the road of trying to hurt you. You are confirming it is safe to move.

In plain English, verification means confirming important claims through a trusted source before taking action. If a message says your bank account is locked, you verify through the official app or website. If a vendor says banking details changed, you verify through a known vendor contact. If a family member says they need emergency money, you verify through a known number or family phrase. If an executive requests a payment, you verify through the approved internal process.

Verification moves trust away from appearance and toward proof.

That move is necessary because blind trust can now be manufactured. Fake profiles can borrow the look of a real person. Fake voices can borrow emotion. Fake emails can borrow a company's branding. Fake invoices can borrow a vendor relationship. Fake family emergencies can borrow panic. Fake documents can borrow legal language. Fake investment opportunities can borrow hope. Fake authority can borrow fear.

A person can be honest. The message using their name may not be.

That sentence lets us verify without turning the person into the problem. If I receive a strange message from someone I know, verification does not mean I distrust that person. It means I understand someone else may be using their name, account, voice, phone number, profile, or relationship. In that moment, verification protects both of us.

Verification protects families because it gives people a way to pause during fear. It protects businesses because it stops money, access, payroll, and authority from moving on appearance alone. It protects customers because it reduces fake pages and impersonation. It protects employees because they do not have to guess alone. It protects leaders because it creates a record of who approved what. It protects public-facing people because it keeps impersonators from speaking unchecked.

Verification creates confidence.

The highest-risk actions should always be verified. Money movement. Password resets. Vendor banking changes. Payroll changes. Legal threats. Identity requests. Access requests. Admin changes. Emergency messages. Investment offers. Job offers. Brand deals. Public statements. Family emergencies. Account recovery requests. Social media ownership changes. Domain changes. Payment processor changes. Requests for codes. Requests for secrecy.

If the action can move money, expose identity, change access, damage reputation, create legal risk, or affect family safety, verify it.

The channel matters. Use a separate trusted channel for anything important. Call a known phone number. Use the official app. Type the official website manually. Use a pre-agreed family phrase. Contact the known vendor representative. Follow the internal escalation process. Require a second approver. Use a secure portal. Contact a trusted recovery person. Confirm with a verified executive contact. Use an official legal contact. Follow a documented payment workflow.

The key is that the verification channel must not be controlled by the suspicious message.

This rule is essential: do not verify the message using the phone number, link, email address, portal, attachment, or contact information inside the suspicious message.

That is how scams trap people. The fake bank alert gives you a fake support number. The fake legal notice gives you a fake attorney contact. The fake vendor email gives you a fake callback number. The fake investor process gives you a fake portal. The fake family emergency gives you a new number and tells you not to call anyone else. If the message provides the path to verification, the attacker may control the path.

Real verification happens outside the message.

Families need simple verification habits before fear takes over. Create an emergency phrase. Call back known numbers. Never send money based only on panic. Protect older relatives. Teach children to ask before sharing information. Do not shame someone for checking. Have a plan for fake emergencies. Verify unusual requests through another family member. Teach everyone not to share codes. Avoid reacting only to voice or video.

A family verification plan should feel protective, not suspicious. If a child really needs help, the emergency phrase helps the family respond faster with confidence. If an older relative receives a fake bank call, the plan gives them permission to pause. If a parent hears a frightening voice message, the plan gives them a second step before panic takes control.

Businesses need verification rules because money, access, authority, payroll, vendors, and customers move through people. A business cannot rely on every employee recognizing every fake message under pressure. It needs process.

Vendor change verification. Payment approval rules. Dual approval for finance and payroll. Known-channel callbacks. Access request reviews. Documented escalation. No-shame reporting. Evidence preservation. Clear authority rules. Owner and executive verification too. Admin change approval. Payroll-change confirmation. Legal-threat escalation. Customer-data request review.

No one should be above verification. Not even the owner.

That may challenge some leaders, but it is one of the most important cultural shifts in modern security. If the owner can bypass every rule, then anyone impersonating the owner will try to bypass every rule. If executives are allowed to move money by voice, email, or text without verification, then fake executive messages become more dangerous. If leadership treats verification as something only employees must do, the business creates a vulnerability at the top.

A strong leader says, "We verify because the threat has changed, not because we distrust our people."

That line matters because verification should not feel like punishment. It should feel like protection. A good leader makes verification normal before a crisis, not personal during one.

Public-facing people need verification even more because their names, faces, voices, brands, and audiences can be copied. A public speaker, creator, executive, founder, or high-profile professional needs official channels, verified contact points, controlled brand-deal processes, fake-profile monitoring, a crisis statement plan, trusted legal, public-relations, and security contacts, clear public communication rules, audience warnings about impersonators, a documented endorsement process, a secure business inquiry path, and an evidence process for fake content.

If your name, face, voice, audience, or reputation has value, verification becomes protection.

This is how verification stops social engineering. Social engineering works by using urgency, fear, authority, secrecy, shame, hope, helpfulness, and confusion. Verification slows the moment down. It gives the person time to ask better questions. Is this real? Is this normal? Can I confirm it another way? Am I being pressured? Am I being isolated? Is someone using authority to bypass process? Is this asking for money, access, identity, or secrecy?

Verification breaks the emotional spell.

Attackers want speed. Verification creates pause. They want secrecy. Verification creates escalation. They want isolation. Verification brings in another person or known channel. They want authority to end the conversation. Verification asks for proof. They want the victim to act inside the attacker's environment. Verification moves the decision outside that environment.

The same principle applies to AI and deepfakes. AI makes appearance less reliable. A voice can be cloned. A video can be faked. A document can be generated. A profile can be built. A screenshot can be fabricated. A message can match someone's tone. If proof depends only on appearance, the attacker has an advantage. Verification moves proof away from appearance and toward trusted process.

That is how people and businesses survive the AI era.

Verified trust is not a feeling. It is a process. It looks like known phone numbers, documented vendor records, passkeys or multi-factor authentication, approval logs, audit trails, recovery contacts, official account lists, role-based access, payment-change workflows, incident timelines, family emergency phrases, executive callback rules, secure portals, trusted legal contacts, vendor master records, and evidence preservation.

Some of those controls may sound formal, but they all serve the same purpose: they create proof outside the moment of pressure.

A family emergency phrase creates proof outside panic. A known vendor contact creates proof outside a suspicious invoice. A second approval creates proof outside one person's rushed decision. An audit trail creates proof after the fact. A secure portal creates proof outside a link in a message. A trusted legal contact creates proof outside a threatening attachment. A vendor master record creates proof outside a changed email thread.

One helpful way to think about this is a verification ladder. Low-risk actions need basic caution. Medium-risk actions need confirmation. High-risk actions need independent verification. Critical actions need documented approval and evidence.

Low-risk actions might include reading a newsletter, checking a normal message, or browsing a known site. Medium-risk actions might include opening a document, responding to a customer request, or updating non-sensitive information. High-risk actions include changing payment details, resetting passwords, sharing personal information, granting access, or responding to unusual requests. Critical actions include moving money, changing payroll, approving legal action, changing admin access, responding to extortion, issuing public statements, approving emergency transfers, changing domain settings, or modifying account recovery.

The higher the risk, the stronger the verification.

We also have to be honest about the danger of over-verifying everything. People cannot verify every tiny detail. If verification becomes exhausting, people will ignore it. A security process that treats every message like a crisis will train people to bypass the process. Smart verification is targeted.

Do not make people verify every ordinary detail. Make them verify the things that can hurt them: money, identity, access, payroll, legal threats, emergency requests, public reputation, business authority, recovery settings, admin changes, vendor banking, and account control.

That is the difference between discipline and paranoia. Paranoia sees danger everywhere and becomes impossible to maintain. Discipline identifies the moments that matter and protects them consistently.

Readers can begin with a personal verification audit. Who controls your email recovery? Who has access to your phone plan? Which accounts have multi-factor authentication? Which family members know emergency rules? Which public profiles are real? Which old accounts still exist? Which apps have permissions? Which devices are logged in? Where are recovery codes stored? Which accounts use reused passwords? Which social media accounts are public? Which data broker listings expose you? Which accounts control money or identity?

Business owners need a business verification audit. Who can move money? Who can change payroll? Who can approve vendors? Who owns the domain? Who controls social media? Who has admin access? Who still has old access? Which vendor contacts are official? Which backups work? Which incident contacts are real? Who can access cloud files? Who can access customer data? Who has finance permissions? Which contractors still have access? Which payment workflows require approval? Which former employees remain active?

A business that cannot answer those questions is not fully in control of its own trust system. That does not mean the business is doomed. It means the business has work to do. The goal is not perfection. The goal is visibility, control, and documented proof where it matters.

Verification turns uncertainty into process.

A fake CEO voice request is stopped because the finance team calls the executive through a known number before approving the transfer. A fake vendor banking change is stopped because the bookkeeper follows the known-channel confirmation rule. A fake family emergency is stopped because the family uses an emergency phrase. A fake investor process is exposed because the founder verifies outside the documents and website provided by the supposed investor. A fake public profile is caught because the real person's official channels were documented in advance.

These examples show that verification is not complicated. It is disciplined.

This chapter closes Part III because it brings the human side of cybersecurity together. People are not the weakness because they are bad. People become vulnerable when trust has no verification. Human mistakes happen. Smart people get fooled. Privacy exposure gives criminals material. Family members, employees, and vendors can become doorways. AI and deepfakes make appearance less reliable. The thread connecting all of this is trust.

Trust is still necessary. Blind trust is what has become dangerous.

The future does not belong to people who trust no one. A world without trust is not a safer world. It is a broken one. The future belongs to people who know how to verify what matters.

That means families can stay connected without letting panic control decisions. Businesses can move quickly without letting speed override proof. Employees can serve customers without being left alone under pressure. Vendors can be trusted within documented boundaries. Public-facing people can build visibility without letting impersonators define them. Leaders can create cultures where verification is normal, not offensive.

A strong protection system should treat verification as a trust-preservation system. It should classify the risk, check the trust anchor, require second approval where needed, preserve evidence when appropriate, and explain clearly why verification matters. The system should not slow everything down. It should slow the actions that matter.

Trust, but verify what matters. Verify money. Verify access. Verify identity. Verify payment changes. Verify payroll changes. Verify legal threats. Verify emergencies. Verify public statements. Verify anything that can damage your life, your business, your family, your reputation, or your future.

Verification is not rude. Verification is not paranoia. Verification is not the opposite of trust.

Trust is still possible in the digital age, but only when verification becomes part of how we protect it.

Part IV

Protecting Yourself, Your Business, and Your Future

Chapter 19

Your Personal Cybersecurity Baseline

You do not need to become a cybersecurity expert to protect yourself.

That is the first thing I want every reader to understand as we move into this part of the book. Up to this point, we have talked about the world that changed, the attacks hiding in plain sight, and the human side of cybersecurity. Now we have to turn that awareness into protection.

The goal is not to overwhelm you with technical language. The goal is not to make you memorize every threat, every acronym, every tool, or every possible scam. Most people do not need to become analysts to live safer lives online. They need a baseline strong enough that their everyday life is not wide open.

Personal cybersecurity is not about being perfect. It is about closing the obvious doors before criminals find them.

Your baseline is the basic level of protection every person should have before worrying about advanced tools. It is the minimum standard for living safely in a connected world. It means your most important accounts, devices, money, files, identity, and recovery paths are not left exposed. It does not make you invincible. It makes you harder to process.

That phrase matters: harder to process. Many criminals are not looking for the hardest target. They are looking for the easiest one. They are looking for the reused password, the unprotected email, the phone number that can be taken over, the bank account with weak recovery, the social media account with no protection, the old account no one remembers, the app with too much access, the person who clicks because the message looks normal enough.

You may not be able to stop every attempt. But you can stop being wide open.

Start with email and phone.

Email is the front door. The phone is often the master key. Together, they control password resets, verification codes, banking alerts, social media recovery, cloud access, contacts, apps, photos, files, and identity. If a criminal controls your email or phone, they may be able to control everything connected to them.

That is why the personal baseline begins there. Not with advanced software. Not with complex dashboards. Not with a dozen tools you will never use. Start by protecting the accounts and devices that unlock everything else.

Your most important personal accounts should be secured first: email, banking, phone carrier, password manager, social media, cloud storage, tax accounts, insurance portals, medical portals, payment apps, shopping accounts, work accounts, school accounts, government accounts, payroll or benefit accounts, retirement or investment accounts, and any domain or business account if you own a business.

The account that can reset other accounts deserves extra protection.

That rule gives you priority. If you do not know where to begin, ask which accounts control the others. Your email may reset your bank. Your phone may receive the code. Your password manager may hold the keys. Your phone carrier may control the number used for recovery. Your cloud storage may hold identity documents. Your social media may control your reputation. Those accounts are not ordinary. They are part of your control center.

Now we need to talk about passwords again, but in a practical way. Every important account needs a unique password. Your email password should never be reused. Your banking password should never be reused. Your password manager password should never be reused. Your business passwords should never be shared. Your social media passwords should be unique. Your cloud storage password should be unique.

Use a password manager instead of memory.

That is not because people are lazy or careless. It is because modern life has too many accounts for memory to be a safe security system. If you try to remember everything, you will probably reuse passwords, weaken passwords, write them down in unsafe places, or create patterns criminals can guess. A password manager helps you use stronger unique passwords without turning security into a memory contest.

And never share codes.

A verification code is not just a number. It may be the key to the account. If someone calls, texts, emails, or direct messages you and asks for a code, stop. A real support person should not need you to read them the code that proves control of your account. If you did not request the code, treat it like a warning. If you receive a login prompt you did not request, do not approve it just to make the notification disappear.

Use multi-factor authentication on critical accounts. Text-message codes are better than nothing, but they are weaker than other options because phone numbers can be targeted. Authenticator apps are stronger. Passkeys or security keys are stronger where available. Recovery codes must be protected because they can bypass normal login protection.

Multi-factor authentication is not magic, but it is one of the simplest ways to make an account harder to take over.

For your email account, the baseline is clear. Use a unique strong password. Turn on multi-factor authentication. Review the recovery email and phone number. Check forwarding rules. Check logged-in devices. Remove unknown connected apps. Review filters and mailbox rules. Log out old sessions. Watch for password reset alerts. Separate personal and business email where possible. Do not store sensitive documents forever just because email feels convenient.

Your email account should be treated like a front door, a safe, and a master key.

If that sounds serious, it should. Your inbox may contain bank alerts, tax documents, contracts, medical messages, passwords resets, travel details, receipts, family information, cloud links, business conversations, social media recovery notices, and old attachments you forgot were there. If someone gets inside, they are not only reading messages. They may be reading the map of your life.

Your phone baseline is just as important. Lock the phone. Update it. Review apps. Remove unused apps. Review permissions. Protect the phone carrier account. Use strong authentication. Do not share verification codes. Do not approve random prompts. Know what to do if your number is taken over. Avoid storing recovery codes in screenshots. Remove old devices from accounts. Use official app stores. Be careful with unknown links in text messages.

Your phone is not just a device. It is part of your identity system.

Most people carry banking, email, social media, work apps, authentication prompts, photos, contacts, cloud files, calendars, payment apps, and location history in one device. That convenience is powerful. It also means the phone deserves more protection than people usually give it. If your phone becomes the recovery path for everything, then protecting the phone carrier account becomes part of protecting your identity.

Banking and financial accounts need their own baseline. Use unique passwords. Turn on multi-factor authentication. Enable account alerts. Use official apps. Do not click bank links from text messages. Avoid banking on public Wi-Fi when possible. Review transactions. Separate personal and business banking. Freeze or lock cards quickly if needed. Check connected payment apps. Review authorized devices. Keep bank fraud numbers saved from official sources, not from messages that arrive during a crisis.

Money accounts should never rely on reused passwords or casual recovery settings.

Your bank may have fraud systems, but your personal habits still matter. Do not assume the bank will catch everything. Do not assume a text message is real because it includes the bank's name. Do not assume a caller is legitimate because caller ID looks familiar. If money is involved, go through the official app, official website, or a number you already know is real.

Social media also belongs in your personal baseline because social media is not only entertainment. It is identity, reputation, and research material for criminals. Lock down privacy settings. Use unique passwords. Turn on multi-factor authentication. Remove unknown connected apps. Review who can see posts. Stop posting live travel or location. Watch for impersonation. Know official recovery options. Avoid sharing family details or security-question clues. Separate public and private accounts if needed. Review old posts. Protect business pages and admin roles.

If someone takes over your social media, they may not only embarrass you. They may message your contacts, scam your audience, damage your reputation, steal business opportunities, or impersonate you to people who already trust your name. For public-facing people and business owners, social media accounts can become business assets. Treat them that way.

Cloud storage is another personal baseline area. Use a unique password. Turn on multi-factor authentication. Review shared links. Remove old shared folders. Do not store sensitive documents in open folders. Separate personal and business files. Back up important files. Know who has access. Remove former collaborators. Review connected apps. Protect recovery settings.

Cloud storage can become a filing cabinet for your entire life. Treat it that way.

Many people use cloud storage because it is easy. Photos sync automatically. Documents move across devices. Family files are shared. Business folders are created quickly. Links are sent without thinking. Over time, old folders, old links, and old collaborators remain active. That is exposure. A shared folder you forgot about can still be accessed. A link you sent months ago may still work. A former collaborator may still see files long after the project ended.

Review the doors you forgot were open.

Apps are another part of the baseline. Every app is a door into some part of your life. Some doors are necessary. Some are not. Review which apps can access your location, contacts, photos, microphone, camera, files, Bluetooth, calendar, messages, health data, and payment information. If an app does not need access, remove the access.

Convenience should not mean unlimited permission.

This does not mean every app is bad. It means every permission should have a reason. A weather app may not need your contacts. A photo editing app may not need your location all the time. A game may not need access to your microphone. A random app you used once should not keep access forever. Your phone should not become a collection of forgotten doors.

Old accounts are forgotten doors too.

Find old accounts. Delete what you do not use. Change reused passwords. Remove saved payment methods. Close abandoned subscriptions. Remove old apps. Review old email recovery connections. Delete old cloud shares. Remove old devices. Check old social media profiles.

An account you forgot can still be used against you.

People often say, "That old account does not matter." Maybe the account itself does not matter. But the password may matter if it was reused. The email address may matter if it connects to other accounts. The saved card may matter. The old phone number may matter. The public profile may matter. Criminals do not care whether you care about the account. They care whether it gives them another door.

Updates are another basic protection. Updates close known holes. Delaying updates leaves old doors open. You do not need to understand every patch note. You need to understand that criminals often look for systems that are behind.

Turn on automatic updates where reasonable. Update phones, computers, browsers, apps, routers, and security tools. If a device can no longer receive updates, understand that it may not be safe for sensitive activity. Old devices may still work, but working is not the same as secure.

Public Wi-Fi requires common sense. Public Wi-Fi is not automatically evil, but it is not where you should handle your most sensitive business. Avoid sensitive logins when possible. Use mobile data for banking or payroll if available. Avoid banking, payroll, or admin work on public networks. Do not accept random prompts. Use a trusted VPN only if appropriate. Keep file sharing off. Avoid connecting to unknown networks. Be careful with hotel, airport, and cafe Wi-Fi.

The issue is not that you can never use public Wi-Fi. The issue is knowing what not to do there. Checking the weather is not the same as approving payroll. Reading a public article is not the same as logging into banking. The more sensitive the action, the more careful the connection should be.

Every person also needs a personal recovery plan.

A recovery plan is not fear. It is preparation. Know how to recover email. Know how to contact your phone carrier. Know where recovery codes are stored. Know your bank fraud contact information. Know how to access accounts from a backup device. Know your trusted contacts. Know which accounts are most critical. Know how to preserve evidence. Know what to do if attacked. Know how to lock cards. Know how to revoke sessions. Know how to warn contacts if impersonation occurred.

The worst time to figure out recovery is after the account is already gone.

If something feels wrong, the first step is not panic. Stop. Do not click more. Do not reply. Do not delete evidence. Preserve screenshots, messages, links, and timestamps. Change passwords from a safe device if needed. Log out all sessions. Check recovery settings. Contact the bank, platform, or carrier if needed. Warn contacts if impersonation occurred. Watch for follow-up scams. Document what happened.

The goal is to contain first, then recover.

Too many people try to fix everything while still standing inside the attack. They keep clicking. They keep replying. They delete the message. They use the compromised device. They change one password and assume everything is solved. Slow down. Preserve proof. Move to a safe device. Protect the accounts that control recovery. Then work outward.

The biggest personal cybersecurity mistakes are usually not exotic. One password everywhere. No multi-factor authentication. Ignoring account alerts. Sharing codes. Clicking urgent links. Posting too much. Using old devices. Leaving accounts logged in. Using one email for everything. Trusting caller ID. Trusting voice or video without verification. Saving sensitive documents everywhere. Keeping old accounts alive. Giving apps too much access. Ignoring recovery settings.

Most personal cybersecurity improvement starts by closing the obvious doors.

That is why a personal baseline checklist matters. Not as a complicated manual, but as a starting point.

Protect your email: unique password, multi-factor authentication, recovery review, forwarding-rule check, logged-in device review.

Protect your phone: lock it, update it, review apps, protect the carrier account, do not share codes.

Protect your passwords: use a password manager, use unique passwords, do not share critical passwords, do not reuse passwords on important accounts.

Protect your money: use multi-factor authentication, alerts, official apps, transaction review, and no banking links from text messages.

Protect your identity: limit oversharing, protect recovery information, monitor suspicious messages, and review public exposure.

Protect your social media: turn on multi-factor authentication, adjust privacy settings, monitor impersonation, and stop posting live location details.

Protect your files: secure cloud storage, review shared links, back up important files, and separate personal and business documents.

Protect your family: talk about scams, create emergency phrases, protect children's privacy, and watch for elder scams without shame.

Protect your recovery paths: secure recovery codes, trusted contacts, phone carrier access, backup device access, and official bank or platform contacts.

This checklist should not make you feel overwhelmed. It should make the problem smaller. Here are the doors. Here is how to close them. Start with the ones that matter most.

If you only do one thing this week, protect your email and phone. If you do two more things, turn on multi-factor authentication for your bank and use unique passwords for critical accounts. If you do one more thing after that, review app permissions and old accounts. Do not wait for the perfect weekend to fix everything. Start where the risk is highest.

This is where modern protection systems should help ordinary people. A person should not have to become a cybersecurity analyst to know what matters. A good personal security system should explain account risk, device safety, scam guidance, email and password risk, multi-factor authentication reminders, phone-security steps, social media privacy warnings, app permissions, family protection, recovery steps, evidence preservation, and plain-English next actions.

The user should be able to open the system and answer three simple questions: Am I safe enough today? What needs attention? What should I do next?

That is the direction personal cybersecurity needs to move. Less noise. More clarity. Fewer panic alerts. More useful guidance. The average person does not need another dashboard full of technical language. They need to know what is open, what matters most, and what to fix first.

A personal cybersecurity baseline should be treated as a posture, not a one-time setup. Accounts change. Phones change. Apps change. Recovery settings change. Old accounts return. Data broker listings come back. New scams appear. Family members get new devices. Banks change processes. Businesses add tools. That means the baseline should be reviewed, not forgotten.

Security is not something you set once and never touch again. It is maintenance, like locking doors, checking smoke detectors, updating insurance, or changing batteries. It is part of modern life now.

The good news is that the baseline is achievable. You do not need to do everything at once. You do not need expensive enterprise tools to begin. You do not need to understand every attack. You need to protect the accounts that matter, reduce obvious exposure, use better authentication, stop sharing codes, update devices, review permissions, clean up old accounts, and know how to recover if something goes wrong.

That is not perfection. That is preparation.

The goal is to become harder to process. Harder to trick. Harder to take over. Harder to impersonate. Harder to rush. Harder to use as an easy doorway. The criminal may still try, but your baseline forces them to work harder, and many criminals prefer easier targets.

Personal cybersecurity is not about being perfect. It is about closing the obvious doors before criminals find them.

Your baseline is not the ceiling of your protection. It is the floor - the minimum standard for living safely in a connected world.

Chapter 20

Building a Business Cybersecurity Baseline

A business cybersecurity baseline is not about buying every tool on the market.

That is where many owners get stuck. They hear the word cybersecurity and immediately imagine expensive software, technical dashboards, consultants, long policies, and systems they do not have time to understand. So they delay. They tell themselves they will handle it when the company gets bigger, when cash flow improves, when the next hire comes in, when the next contract closes, or when they finally have time to sit down and figure it all out.

But cybersecurity is not waiting for your business to become convenient. It is already part of how your company operates. It is part of how money moves. It is part of payroll. It is part of email. It is part of customer trust. It is part of employee access. It is part of vendor relationships. It is part of your reputation. It is part of whether the business can keep moving when something goes wrong.

So when I talk about a business cybersecurity baseline, I am not talking about turning every business owner into an IT department. I am talking about the minimum operating discipline every business needs before it tries to get fancy. At the most basic level, a business owner should be able to answer a few plain questions without opening ten different systems or calling five different people. What do we use? Who has access? What can they touch? What must be protected? What happens if we lose access? What happens if money gets redirected? What happens if a vendor is impersonated? What happens if payroll is attacked? What happens if customer data is exposed?

That is not an IT manual. That is business survival.

A lot of business owners still think cybersecurity begins with firewalls, antivirus, and technical settings. Those things matter, but the real risk often lives in ordinary decisions. Who can approve a payment? Who can change payroll? Who owns the domain name? Who controls the company email? Who can post as the business? Who can access customer records? Who can open vendor attachments? Who can reset passwords? Who can move money when the owner is traveling or distracted?

Those questions do not sound technical because they are not only technical. They are operational. Cybersecurity has moved into the daily flow of business. If you run a company, cybersecurity is no longer a separate topic that belongs somewhere in the back office. It is how the business protects trust, money, people, and continuity.

Start by protecting what keeps the business alive. For most companies, that means money, email, payroll, customer records, employee records, bank accounts, vendor relationships, the domain name, the website, social media pages, payment processors, cloud files, accounting software, tax records, contracts, insurance documents, legal records, admin accounts, and brand reputation. You do not have to protect everything at the same level on day one, but you do have to know what would hurt the business most if it were stolen, locked, copied, redirected, or used against you.

The rule is simple: protect what criminals can use to stop the business, steal money, impersonate the business, or damage trust.

That rule helps cut through the noise. The account that controls other accounts is high risk. The email account that receives password resets is high risk. The bank login is high risk. The payroll system is high risk. The domain registrar is high risk. The social media admin account that speaks to customers is high risk. The cloud storage folder with contracts, tax records, payroll files, and customer information is high risk. The payment processor is high risk. The owner's phone may be high risk because it approves access to all of it.

Once you understand that, the baseline becomes clearer. You secure the owner email and finance email first. You secure payroll, banking, accounting, the domain registrar, website hosting, social media admin accounts, cloud storage, customer systems, payment processors, tax accounts, insurance portals, HR systems, and admin dashboards. You do not do this because every account is equally interesting. You do it because some accounts can unlock the rest of the business.

Business passwords need a grown-up standard. No shared passwords for critical systems. Every critical account needs a unique password. A business password manager should be used instead of spreadsheets, email drafts, text messages, sticky notes, or shared chats. When someone leaves, access has to be removed immediately. Verification codes should never be shared. A password is not just a login in business. A password can be money, customer data, payroll, reputation, or control.

Multi-factor authentication has to be treated the same way. The owner account needs it. Admin accounts need it. Finance, payroll, HR, email, cloud storage, domain registration, website hosting, social media, payment processors, accounting software, customer systems, tax accounts, and insurance portals need it. Text-message codes are better than nothing, but stronger options such as authenticator apps, passkeys, or security keys should be used where possible, especially on the accounts closest to money, identity, and administration.

And if a login prompt appears that no one requested, do not approve it. If a code arrives that no one asked for, do not share it. In a business, a code is not just a number. It may be the key to payroll, bank access, customer records, or the company domain.

Employee access is where many companies become messy. The question should not be, do we trust this person? The better question is, what access does this role actually need? A bookkeeper may need invoice access, but not social media ownership. A marketing contractor may need campaign assets, but not payroll. A receptionist may need scheduling, but not banking. A manager may need customer records, but not domain administration. Trust is personal. Access should be operational.

That is the idea behind role-based access and least privilege. Give people the access they need to do the job, not unlimited access because it was easier during setup. Review access regularly. Use separate admin accounts. Avoid shared logins. Set expiration dates for contractors. Document who has access to what. Separate finance, payroll, HR, and administrative authority where possible. When sensitive actions happen, the business should know who did what and why.

Offboarding is one of the places where discipline matters most. When someone leaves, access ends before the relationship fully ends, not days or weeks later. That is not cold. It is responsible. It protects the company, and it protects the former employee from being blamed later for activity that happened after they left.

A clean offboarding process does not need drama. It needs a checklist behind the scenes, even if the chapter does not read like one. The email account is disabled or transferred. Sessions are revoked. Cloud access is removed. Payroll, HR, customer systems, social media, vendor portals, and admin rights are closed. Company devices are recovered. Shared passwords are rotated if any still exist. File ownership is transferred. Connected apps are reviewed. The closure is documented. A delayed offboarding process is an open door.

Vendors need the same kind of discipline. A vendor relationship is not proof that every vendor message is real. Trusted vendors can be impersonated. Trusted vendors can be compromised. Trusted vendors can send invoices, request access, provide software updates, handle payroll, manage IT, run accounting, support marketing, process payments, host websites, manage benefits, handle legal documents, or touch customer data. That means vendor trust needs boundaries.

The business should know its real vendor contacts. It should have a normal invoice process. It should verify payment changes through a known channel. It should limit vendor access to what the vendor actually needs. It should review vendor permissions. It should remove vendor access when the work ends. It should require stronger authentication where possible. It should not rely only on an email thread when banking details change. A vendor email can be compromised, and a familiar-looking invoice can still be a trap.

Money movement deserves special rules. No one message should be enough to move money. That one sentence can save a business. If banking instructions change, verify outside email. If payroll information changes, verify through a known process. If an urgent payment appears to come from the owner, confirm through a trusted channel. If a legal threat demands immediate payment, escalate before acting. Use dual approval where the risk is high. Set payment limits where possible. Turn on fraud alerts. Keep bank contacts saved from official sources. Know how to freeze payments in an emergency.

This is not bureaucracy. It is how a business keeps normal operations from becoming a criminal workflow.

Email is another critical piece of the baseline because business email often controls money, access, customers, and recovery. A business should use professional domain email rather than running company operations through one personal account. Owner and finance accounts should be protected like critical infrastructure. Multi-factor authentication should be required. Forwarding rules and mailbox rules should be reviewed. Old users should be removed. Suspicious logins should be taken seriously. Staff should be trained to recognize phishing. Personal and business email should be separated where possible. Sensitive documents should not live forever in email just because it is convenient.

The same thinking applies to domain names, websites, and social media. A stolen domain or social page can become a public business hostage situation. The business should know who owns the domain, who controls the registrar, who has access to hosting, and how recovery works. Multi-factor authentication should be on the registrar and hosting accounts. Social media admin roles should be limited. A business page should not be controlled only by one person's personal account. Official channels should be documented, fake pages should be monitored, recovery contacts should be protected, and former staff should be removed from public-facing accounts.

Cloud files and documents need ownership too. A shared folder can become a data leak if nobody owns it. The business should know where contracts, tax records, invoices, payroll files, customer records, insurance documents, and legal files live. Shared links should be reviewed. Old collaborators should be removed. Personal and business files should be separated. Critical documents should be backed up. Public links should be limited. Folder permissions should be checked. Former contractors should not keep access months after a project ended.

Devices matter because devices are doors. A laptop is not just a laptop if it contains customer data. A phone is not just a phone if it approves payroll, bank access, or admin logins. The business should keep devices updated, require screen locks, remove old devices, use endpoint protection, and have rules for employee devices. Owner, finance, and payroll phones deserve stronger protection because they often approve the most sensitive actions. Sensitive business work should not be done casually on public Wi-Fi. If company data sits on personal devices, the business needs rules for how that data is protected and removed when the relationship ends.

Backups are not optional. They are business continuity. The question is not just whether a backup exists. The question is whether it works. What gets backed up? Where is it backed up? Who can access it? Has recovery been tested? Is cloud sync being mistaken for backup? Which systems must come back first? Are backups protected from ransomware? Are the critical documents recoverable? A backup only matters if it can restore what the business actually needs under pressure.

The worst time to test recovery is during a crisis. By then everyone is tired, scared, and rushed. A business should know before the crisis whether the files can come back, whether the backup account is protected, and who has authority to start recovery.

Every business also needs an incident plan, but it does not have to be fancy. It has to be usable when people are stressed. The plan should make clear who to call, what to freeze, how to preserve evidence, how to contact the bank, how to contact platforms, how to contact phone carriers, how to contact vendors, who can speak to customers, who contacts insurance, legal, or security support, how accounts are recovered, how the timeline is documented, how payroll and payment changes are stopped during the crisis, and which communication channel is trusted if email is compromised.

If that sounds like a lot, think of it this way: during a cyber incident, the business does not need a beautiful binder. It needs to know what happens next. Who makes decisions? Who has the bank number? Who can freeze payments? Who can restore accounts? Who tells employees what to do? Who speaks to customers if customers need to know? Who preserves the evidence before someone deletes the message out of embarrassment?

Employee training should be plain English and repeated regularly. Employees need to know how phishing works, how vendor and payment verification works, why codes are never shared, how suspicious messages are reported, how to handle attachments, how to escalate legal threats, how to protect customer information, and what to do after a mistake. Training should not be built around shame. It should be built around practice.

People do not rise to the level of policy during panic. They fall to the level of practice.

That is why reporting culture matters. Employees should never feel punished for reporting quickly. Fast reporting protects the business. Shame protects the attacker. If someone clicks something, shares something, or notices something strange, the first goal is containment, not blame. A no-shame reporting culture makes the business safer because problems surface faster.

Compliance and insurance also belong in this conversation, but they should be kept practical. Insurance may require certain controls. Compliance may require documentation. Claims may depend on evidence. Contracts may require proof of safeguards. Customers may want to know what happened and what was done. If controls are not documented before something goes wrong, they may be harder to prove afterward.

Small businesses and enterprise organizations do not need the exact same baseline, but they do need the same discipline at different levels. A small business needs simple controls that people actually follow. A growing company needs documented governance. An enterprise-level organization needs formal access control, audit logs, incident command, vendor risk management, continuity planning, executive visibility, and legal or compliance documentation.

That is why the protection model has to grow with the business. A smaller operating company needs help seeing accounts, employees, vendors, payments, devices, reporting, and recovery without drowning in complexity. A larger organization needs governance, incident command, evidence preservation, vendor risk, executive-level controls, formal access, audit logs, recovery orchestration, and crisis communication. Home protection belongs to the person. Small business protection belongs to the operating company. Enterprise protection belongs to the organization that cannot afford confusion when something goes wrong.

The biggest business cybersecurity mistakes are usually ordinary. Shared passwords. No multi-factor authentication. Former employees still active. No vendor verification. Untested backups. Too many disconnected tools. The owner controlling everything through one phone. Personal email used for business. No incident plan. No employee training. No access review. No payment approval rules. No documentation. No domain protection. No social media ownership plan. No reporting culture. No recovery process.

Most business risk begins with ordinary gaps.

A business owner does not have to fix every gap in one day. Start with the doors that matter most. Protect money. Protect email. Protect employee access. Protect vendors. Protect payroll. Protect customer data. Protect devices. Protect cloud files. Protect the domain and social media. Protect backups. Protect incident response.

But even that should not become another overwhelming checklist taped to a wall and ignored. The real goal is awareness and discipline. Know your doors. Know your keys. Know who can use them. Know what actions require verification. Know what gets frozen during a crisis. Know how to recover. Know how to prove what happened.

That is what a business cybersecurity baseline is. It is not a technology shopping list. It is a way of operating so that trust, money, people, and reputation are not left exposed.

A secure business is not one that never faces risk. Every connected business faces risk. A secure business knows its doors, controls its access, verifies high-risk actions, and can recover when something goes wrong.

Your business baseline is not bureaucracy. It is the operating discipline that keeps trust, money, people, and reputation protected.

Chapter 21

Fewer Tools, Fewer Doors

Every tool is a door.

That may sound too simple, but it is one of the most important ideas a business owner can understand. Every app has a login. Every login has a password. Every password has a recovery path. Every recovery path can be attacked. Every vendor has some kind of relationship with the business. Every integration connects one system to another. Every dashboard becomes another place where something can be missed, misused, forgotten, or taken over.

That does not mean tools are bad. A modern business needs technology. Payroll needs a system. Banking needs a system. Accounting needs a system. Customer records, cloud files, scheduling, payments, email, marketing, insurance, taxes, social media, project management, HR, vendor portals, customer support, and contracts all need somewhere to live. The problem is not that businesses use tools. The problem is that businesses keep adding tools without controlling the doors those tools create.

You do not protect a business by collecting tools. You protect a business by controlling the doors those tools create.

This is where many companies get themselves into trouble. A business starts small, and every new problem gets solved with another app. One tool handles invoices. Another handles payroll. Another handles scheduling. Another handles payments. Another holds customer records. Another stores files. Another manages social media. Another handles email marketing. Another tracks projects. Another handles forms. Another handles contracts. Each decision makes sense at the time. The owner is not trying to create chaos. The owner is trying to get through the day.

But after a while, the business is not running on a clean operating system. It is running on a pile of disconnected doors.

The owner may not know who has admin access anymore. The bookkeeper may not know which invoice process is official. Employees may not know whether files belong in the cloud drive, the CRM, the project board, the email thread, or the shared folder someone created two years ago. A vendor may send messages through a portal, email, text, and a support desk. A customer may receive payment links from more than one place. A former contractor may still have access to a folder nobody checks. A social media page may be controlled through someone's personal account. The domain may be tied to an old email address. The backup may depend on a system nobody has tested.

That is not just inconvenient. It is a cybersecurity risk.

Tool sprawl is what happens when a business keeps adding systems faster than it adds control. The more disconnected systems a business has, the harder it becomes to know who has access, what data is stored where, which accounts are critical, which vendors are connected, which former employees still have access, which tools have multi-factor authentication, which dashboards can move money, which systems hold customer data, and which accounts control recovery during a crisis.

A business cannot protect what it cannot see.

That is why confusion is an attack surface.

Criminals love confusion because confusion slows people down in the wrong way. It makes employees unsure which system is official. It makes invoices harder to verify. It makes access harder to remove. It makes fake vendor requests harder to catch. It makes alerts easier to ignore because there are too many of them. It makes recovery harder because no one knows which account controls what. A clean system is easier to protect. A messy system gives criminals places to hide.

This is especially hard on small businesses because most small businesses do not create tool sprawl on purpose. They add tools one by one to solve immediate problems. There is nothing wrong with that at the beginning. A business needs to move. It needs to invoice customers. It needs to schedule appointments. It needs to pay people. It needs to market. It needs to collect money. It needs to store documents. But if every problem creates another disconnected system, eventually the owner is not managing a business anymore. The owner is managing a maze.

And in a maze, mistakes become easier.

Employees feel that maze too. When there are too many tools, people create shortcuts. They save passwords badly because they cannot remember which login goes where. They reuse passwords because every platform asks for another one. They move files through personal email because the official system feels too slow. They use unauthorized apps because the approved tool does not do what they need. They share links too widely because permissions are confusing. They ignore alerts because alerts come from everywhere. They take screenshots because that feels easier than exporting a record properly. They store customer data in the wrong place because nobody explained where the official place is.

Most of those shortcuts do not come from bad intentions. They come from friction. When the system is too complicated, people build their own paths through it. Those paths may help them finish the task, but they can also create risk the business cannot see.

This is the plain-English version of shadow IT. It means people are using tools for work that the business did not officially approve, secure, or track. It might be a personal drive folder, a free scheduling app, a private email account, a messaging app, a note-taking tool, a spreadsheet with customer data, a file-sharing link, or a random AI tool someone tried because it made the work faster. The danger is simple. If the business does not know the tool exists, the business cannot protect it, audit it, recover it, or remove access when someone leaves.

Customers and vendors can get pulled into the confusion too. If a business has too many payment links, too many invoice formats, too many support channels, and too many staff members using different systems, it becomes harder for outsiders to know what is real. That creates room for impersonation. A fake invoice is more believable when the real invoice process is already messy. A fake support message is harder to spot when customers already receive messages from several platforms. A fake vendor update blends in when vendors communicate through email, portals, and informal messages without a clear standard.

The more confusing the business looks from the outside, the easier it is for a criminal to imitate normal.

This is why every tool needs to earn its place. A useful tool has a clear purpose, a clear owner, a clear access rule, and a clear recovery plan. An unmanaged doorway is a tool nobody fully controls. The difference is not whether the tool is useful. A payroll system is useful. A payment processor is useful. A CRM is useful. A cloud drive is useful. But if nobody knows who has admin access, what email controls recovery, whether former employees have been removed, how changes are approved, or how the business gets back in after a lockout, that useful tool has become an unmanaged door.

A tool is not only software. It is a commitment.

When a business adds a tool, it adds responsibility. It adds another vendor. Another login. Another admin account. Another recovery email. Another integration. Another place for customer information. Another place for invoices. Another employee permission. Another system to offboard. Another place something can break. That does not mean the tool should not be added. It means the owner should understand what is being added besides convenience.

Before adding a new tool, the business should slow down long enough to ask what problem the tool actually solves. Does the company already have something that does the same job? Does this replace an old tool, or does it just add another door? What data will live inside it? Who owns it? Who needs access? Who can approve access? How does access get removed? Does it support strong authentication? What account controls recovery? What happens if the business loses access? What vendor risk does this create? How will this be documented?

That may sound like a lot of questions, but it is easier to ask them before the tool becomes part of the business than after something goes wrong.

A tool should not be adopted just because it is popular. It should not be added because someone saw an advertisement, received a referral code, or wanted one feature for one project. A tool should support the business. If it does not support the business clearly enough to justify the risk and responsibility, it may not belong there.

This does not mean every company should try to run on one tool for everything. That is not realistic. Some tools specialize for a reason. Payroll, accounting, customer records, legal documents, and communications may need different systems. The goal is not one tool at all costs. The goal is fewer unmanaged doors. Use fewer systems where possible. Choose tools that integrate cleanly. Remove duplicates. Close unused accounts. Stop paying for tools nobody owns. Avoid adding another dashboard unless it truly solves a business problem.

The future of security is not more noise, more dashboards, and more disconnected alerts. The future is a clearer control layer that helps leaders see what the business uses, who has access, what changed, what needs attention, and what should be closed. That is the Aetis idea at its core. Not more chaos. More control.

For a small business, that means the owner should not have to guess which tools exist, who can enter them, which vendors are connected, which payments are risky, which files are exposed, and which employees still have access. For a larger organization, it means governance, audit trails, vendor risk, incident command, continuity, and executive oversight across the whole organization. The level changes as the business grows, but the principle stays the same. You cannot protect the business if you cannot see the doors.

The first cleanup should focus on the easiest open doors. Old accounts. Unused apps. Former employee access. Duplicate tools. Abandoned cloud folders. Old vendor portals. Shared passwords. Unused social media admins. Old contractor accounts. Public file links. Personal email used for business. Tools nobody owns. Apps without multi-factor authentication. Old payment methods. Old integrations. These are the doors criminals hope nobody remembers.

If nobody owns it, nobody is protecting it.

Closing those doors does not require a dramatic transformation. It requires discipline. Pick a tool. Decide whether the business still needs it. Identify the owner. Review who has access. Turn on stronger authentication where possible. Remove old users. Export or preserve what needs to be kept. Close what no longer belongs. Then move to the next tool. A business does not become cleaner because the owner thinks about cleanup once. It becomes cleaner because cleanup becomes part of operations.

The business should also centralize the things that create control. That does not mean dumping every piece of data into one risky place. It means creating one clear control view. The owner should know where the critical accounts are listed. The business should know its vendor records, payment approval process, incident reporting path, password management approach, admin ownership, recovery contacts, employee offboarding process, device inventory, cloud file ownership, domain ownership, social media ownership, backup status, authentication status, and audit trail. The point is not to make the company more complicated. The point is to stop forcing everyone to guess.

Think about a small business that uses one app for invoices, another for payroll, another for HR, another for scheduling, another for customer records, another for cloud storage, another for social media, and another for payments. At first, everything seems fine. Then a fake invoice arrives. Nobody knows whether the invoice came through the official system. The bookkeeper checks email. The owner checks the payment app. An employee checks the CRM. The vendor says they sent it through a portal. The old invoice template is in a shared drive. A former contractor still has access to the cloud folder. The business page is controlled by someone's personal account. The payment instructions changed, but nobody knows who approved the change.

The problem is not only the fake invoice. The problem is the mess.

That mess is what the criminal uses. The fake invoice succeeds because the business cannot quickly prove what normal looks like. When normal is unclear, fake has room to breathe. When official channels are scattered, impersonation becomes easier. When access is unmanaged, former users and compromised accounts can remain invisible. When recovery paths are unknown, a small incident becomes a crisis.

Leaders have to stop buying tools as a substitute for process. A new dashboard does not fix unclear ownership. A new app does not fix poor access control. A new portal does not fix weak payment verification. A new platform does not fix a culture where employees are afraid to report mistakes. Tools can support good process, but they cannot replace it.

That is why every tool should have a purpose. Every tool should have an owner. Every tool should have an access rule. Every tool should have a recovery plan. If it does not, it is not just a tool. It is an unmanaged door.

The owner does not have to become technical to enforce this. The owner has to become disciplined. Before adding something new, ask what it replaces. Before keeping something old, ask who owns it. Before giving someone access, ask what role requires it. Before approving a payment change, ask what process confirms it. Before trusting a dashboard, ask whether the business knows how to recover it if the account is lost.

This is how a business gets simpler without becoming weaker. It does not reject technology. It uses technology intentionally. It does not avoid useful tools. It refuses unmanaged ones. It does not chase every new platform. It makes every platform prove its value. It does not let convenience silently become exposure.

The safest business is not the one with the most tools. It is the one that understands its tools well enough to control them.

That means knowing which doors are open. It means knowing who has the keys. It means knowing which doors can be closed. It means knowing which tools hold money, customer data, payroll information, public reputation, vendor relationships, or recovery control. It means removing the tools that no longer serve the business and strengthening the tools that do.

Fewer tools does not mean less capability. It can mean more clarity. Fewer duplicate systems. Fewer forgotten logins. Fewer exposed files. Fewer former users. Fewer places for fake invoices to hide. Fewer dashboards no one checks. Fewer vendors no one reviews. Fewer recovery paths no one understands. Fewer doors standing open because no one remembered they existed.

There is another layer to this that business owners do not always want to say out loud: tools can become emotional. We buy them because we are trying to look more professional, more organized, more scalable, more prepared. We feel like a new system means the business is maturing. Sometimes it is. But sometimes the tool gives the appearance of maturity without the discipline underneath. A dashboard can make a business look organized while the access behind it is still a mess.

Even security tools can become part of the problem if they are not managed. A company may add one tool for email filtering, another for passwords, another for device protection, another for compliance, another for backups, and another for alerts. Each one may be useful. But if no one knows which alerts matter, who owns the response, what gets logged, and what happens during a real incident, the business has not created security. It has created noise.

More alerts do not automatically mean more protection. More dashboards do not automatically mean more control. More subscriptions do not automatically mean more maturity. If the owner cannot tell what needs attention today, the tools may be working against the business instead of for it.

Tool sprawl also creates cost that is easy to miss. There is the monthly subscription cost, but that is only the obvious part. There is also the cost of training people, remembering logins, managing permissions, reviewing invoices, updating integrations, removing users, handling support tickets, and recovering access when something breaks. A low-cost app can become expensive if it quietly adds confusion to the business.

A business should also be careful with integrations. Integrations are convenient because they let tools talk to each other. But every integration is another connection. If one tool can pull data from another, the business needs to know what data moves, who approved the connection, what permissions were granted, and how to revoke that connection. Many companies connect apps in a hurry and forget them. Months later, an old integration may still have access to information nobody remembers sharing.

Ownership is what keeps tools from drifting. Every tool needs a business owner, not just a user. The owner is the person responsible for knowing why the tool exists, what data it holds, who has access, what integrations are active, how billing works, how recovery works, and what happens if the tool is removed. Without ownership, tools drift. And drift is where risk grows.

Recovery is another reason tools need control. A tool without a recovery plan is a door with a lock no one knows how to open after the key is lost. Who controls the recovery email? What phone number receives the code? Is that phone number still active? Is the account tied to an employee who left? Are backup codes stored somewhere safe? These questions feel boring until the day the business is locked out.

Social media pages and domains are common examples. A business page may have been created years ago through someone's personal account. A domain may be tied to an old personal email. Everything keeps working, so nobody worries about it. Then one day the page is locked, the domain is threatened, or the business cannot prove ownership quickly. The company realizes it never truly controlled the door. It only hoped the door would stay open.

That is why this chapter is not really about fewer tools as much as it is about fewer unknowns. Unknown owners, unknown admins, unknown recovery paths, unknown integrations, unknown former users, unknown data locations, unknown payment links, and unknown official channels create the conditions criminals love. Unknowns are where attackers find opportunity.

The best leaders will not treat simplification as a downgrade. They will treat it as a sign of maturity. Anyone can add another app. Mature businesses know when to say no. They know when to retire a tool. They know when to consolidate. They know when a dashboard is not worth the door it opens. They know when convenience is creating exposure.

The business does not have to become primitive to become safer. It has to become intentional. Use the tools that matter. Govern the tools you keep. Close the tools you do not need. Consolidate where it makes sense. Document ownership. Control access. Protect recovery. Make every tool part of the operating system, not another forgotten door on the side of the building.

That is the point of this chapter. We have made business too complicated, and complexity is now costing us security. The solution is not to panic or throw away every system. The solution is to simplify where possible, govern what remains, and make every tool earn its place.

Every tool is a door. Some doors are necessary. Some doors are useful. Some doors should have been closed a long time ago.

The safest business is not the one with the most tools. It is the one that knows which doors are open, who has the keys, and which doors can be closed.

Chapter 22

Evidence, Logs, and Why Proof Matters

When something goes wrong online, panic is natural.

That is true whether it is a fake invoice, a compromised email account, a suspicious bank transfer, a social media page pretending to be your business, or a ransomware note on a screen. The first reaction is usually not calm. The first reaction is usually fear. People want the scary thing gone. They want the message deleted, the fake profile blocked, the page closed, the password changed, the account recovered, and the problem over as quickly as possible.

That reaction is human. But it can also destroy the very thing you may need most.

Proof.

If something goes wrong, proof is what turns panic into a case, a claim, a report, a recovery path, or a defense. Feelings are not enough. Memory is not enough. Screenshots after everything has already been deleted may not be enough. You may know what happened. You may feel certain about what happened. You may be right about what happened. But if you cannot show it, recovery becomes harder.

The person who can prove the timeline has more power than the person trying to remember what happened.

That is the first thing I want the average reader to understand. After a cyber incident, people are scared, rushed, embarrassed, and confused. They remember pieces, but not always the order. They forget exact times. They forget which link they clicked. They forget the name the caller used. They forget whether the payment request came before or after the login alert. They forget whether the email had an attachment or only a link. They assume they will remember later, but later everything blends together.

Proof creates a record when memory gets shaky. It turns, 'I think this happened,' into, 'Here is what happened.'

That difference matters. It matters to banks. It matters to insurance companies. It matters to law enforcement. It matters to platforms. It matters to vendors. It matters to employees. It matters to customers. It matters to lawyers. It matters to the business owner trying to explain what happened without sounding confused or defensive. Proof gives people options. Without proof, a victim may know the truth but struggle to show it. With proof, they can report, recover, dispute, escalate, defend, and explain.

This is why one of the worst things people do during panic is erase the evidence before they understand the incident.

They delete the message. They clear the alert. They close the tab. They block the account too quickly. They argue with the scammer. They click more links. They lose the timestamp. They forget to screenshot the profile. They change settings without writing down what changed. They try to fix everything before preserving anything. They make the frightening thing disappear, but sometimes the evidence disappears with it.

That does not mean you should leave yourself exposed. It does not mean you should keep talking to a scammer. It does not mean you should keep a dangerous account active. It means you should pause long enough to preserve what matters before you take the next step.

Evidence is not confrontation. Evidence is control.

Preserving evidence does not mean arguing with the attacker. It does not mean replying. It does not mean threatening them. It does not mean pretending to be an investigator or trying to track them yourself. It means calmly saving what may matter before the trail disappears. The evidence may be a message, an email, a phone number, a URL, a timestamp, a profile link, a screenshot, a bank notice, a login alert, a payment confirmation, a password reset email, a forwarding rule, a fake invoice, or a voicemail. If it helps show what happened, when it happened, who was involved, or what changed, preserve it.

Think about a fake invoice. The business receives a message that appears to come from a known vendor. The invoice looks normal. The amount looks familiar. The tone feels professional. The payment instructions have changed, but the change does not look dramatic. Someone pays it. Later the real vendor says they never changed banks and never received the money.

At that moment, proof matters. The business needs the original invoice, the email that delivered it, the sender information, the time it arrived, the payment confirmation, the account information used, the conversation with the real vendor, and the moment the fraud was discovered. The bank may need details. Insurance may need a timeline. The vendor may need proof that the business did not simply ignore payment. The owner may need to show that the process was abused, not that the business acted randomly.

Money movement needs a trail.

The same is true when email is compromised. A person may change the password and feel relieved, but recovery is not only getting back in. If an attacker had access, you need to know what they may have touched. Were forwarding rules created? Were messages deleted? Were recovery settings changed? Were unknown devices connected? Were password reset emails sent? Were messages sent to customers or vendors? Were bank alerts archived or hidden? Were connected apps added?

Those details may matter later. They may explain how the attacker stayed inside the account. They may show whether the attacker read vendor conversations or watched for payment timing. They may show whether other accounts are now at risk. If the only action taken is a password change, important evidence may be missed.

This is where logs come in. Logs are records of what happened. They can show when something happened, where it happened, what account was used, what device was involved, what changed, and sometimes who or what caused it. A log is like a security camera for digital actions. It may not tell the whole story by itself, but it gives banks, platforms, businesses, security teams, and investigators something real to work with.

A business log might show when someone logged in, when a user was added, when a file was accessed, when a payment was approved, when a password changed, when an admin role was assigned, when a device connected, or when a vendor update was made. Without logs, the business may only have guesses. With logs, the business has a timeline.

That timeline can protect the business, but it can also protect the people inside the business.

This part matters because evidence is not only about catching criminals. Evidence also prevents unfair blame. If an employee clicked a message, the evidence can show what the message looked like and whether it was designed to deceive. If an employee approved a payment, the evidence can show whether the vendor account was compromised, whether the request came through a normal channel, whether the approval process was followed, or whether the system failed the employee. If an employee reported quickly, the timeline can show that fast reporting helped contain the damage.

Evidence shifts the conversation from blame to facts.

That is why no-shame reporting and evidence preservation belong together. Fast reporting preserves evidence. Shame destroys it. When people are embarrassed, they hide. When they hide, messages get deleted, alerts disappear, details fade, and attackers get more time. A business that punishes honest reporting may train employees to stay silent. A business that protects fast reporting gets the truth sooner.

The same rule applies in families and personal life. If someone receives a fake emergency message, a suspicious text, a strange login alert, or a call demanding money, the first instinct may be to delete it, block it, and pretend it did not happen. But if the situation involves money, identity, account access, family safety, or impersonation, proof matters. A screenshot, a phone number, a voicemail, a timestamp, a message thread, and a note about what was said may become important if the scam continues, if money moves, or if someone else is targeted.

A suspicious text should not be treated as just an annoyance if it is asking for money, codes, identity, or secrecy. Save the message. Save the number. Note the time. If there was a call, write down what name was used, what they asked for, what threat or urgency they created, and whether there was a voicemail. Stress makes details disappear. Writing them down protects the timeline.

Fake profiles and fake pages create another evidence problem because they can change quickly. A fake page can be renamed. A profile can be deleted. A username can be changed. Posts can disappear. Messages can be unsent. Photos can be swapped. If a fake social media account is impersonating a person or business, do not rely on, 'I saw it.' Capture it. Save the profile link, username, screenshots, posts, messages, dates, and platform report confirmation if you file one. Do not help the fake spread unnecessarily, but do preserve what proves it existed.

This is especially important for public-facing people and businesses. If a fake page uses your name, logo, face, voice, product, event, or business identity, you may need proof for a platform report, a legal notice, a public statement, or a customer warning. If you block too quickly or wait until the page disappears, you may lose the evidence that supports the takedown or shows your audience what was fake.

The same principle applies to ransomware or digital extortion. The ransom note, the file names, the deadline, the payment instructions, the communication channel, the claim that data was stolen, and the first time the business noticed the problem may all matter. That does not mean you should engage with the attacker. It means you should preserve the facts before panic turns everything into a blur.

Memory is unreliable during stress. That is not an insult. It is human biology. When people panic, they forget times. They mix up the order of events. They misremember what they clicked. They forget who they contacted. They assume they will remember later, but later the details blend together. A short note made during the event can be more useful than a polished explanation written days later.

That is what an incident timeline is in plain English. It is a simple record of what happened first, what happened next, who noticed it, what action was taken, who was contacted, what evidence was saved, what changed, and what is still unknown. It does not have to be fancy. It has to be accurate enough to stop everyone from relying on scattered memory.

For an individual, the timeline might be simple. At 9:12 a.m., a text arrived claiming to be the bank. At 9:15, the link was clicked. At 9:17, a login page appeared. At 9:20, the person realized something was wrong. At 9:25, they took screenshots. At 9:30, they went to the bank app directly from a safe device. At 9:40, they changed the password and called the bank using the number from the official website. That is a timeline.

For a business, the timeline may be more involved. A vendor email arrived. A payment change was requested. The bookkeeper approved it. The payment was sent. The real vendor called three days later. The owner froze vendor payment changes. The bank was contacted. The email account was reviewed. The vendor confirmed their account may have been compromised. The business preserved the invoice, email, bank record, and approval message. That is also a timeline.

The timeline does not have to assign blame. It has to create clarity.

Every high-risk action in a business should leave a trail. Payments should leave a trail. Payroll changes should leave a trail. Vendor changes should leave a trail. Admin changes should leave a trail. Access requests should leave a trail. Public statements should leave a trail. Customer-data exports should leave a trail. That does not have to become complicated or bureaucratic. It means decisions should not happen invisibly.

If money, trust, access, identity, or reputation is involved, the business should know who approved it, when it happened, why it happened, and what changed.

Audit trails are not about spying on employees. They are about knowing what happened when trust, money, access, or reputation is at risk. A good audit trail protects the business and the people inside it. It can show that an employee followed process. It can show that a vendor request was abnormal. It can show when access changed. It can show who approved a payment. It can show when an account was compromised. Audit trails replace suspicion with facts.

That is important because suspicion is messy. Facts are cleaner. Without evidence, people start guessing. The owner wonders whether the employee made a mistake. The employee wonders whether the vendor was compromised. The vendor wonders whether the business ignored the correct instructions. The customer wonders whether the business is hiding something. The insurer asks for details. The bank asks for proof. Everyone wants answers, but without evidence the answers come slowly, if they come at all.

With evidence, the business can move differently. It can show the bank what happened. It can give the insurer a timeline. It can support a platform takedown. It can explain to a vendor where the fake instruction came from. It can show customers that the business acted responsibly. It can give legal counsel something real to review. It can improve the process that failed. It can protect employees who reported quickly or followed the rules.

Proof does not solve everything, but it changes the position you are standing in.

The person without proof is often stuck saying, 'You have to believe me.' The person with proof can say, 'Here is the record.'

That is why proof should feel empowering, not intimidating. You do not need to become a forensic expert to preserve useful evidence. You need to slow down enough to save what matters. Screenshot before deleting. Save the email before blocking. Capture the fake profile before reporting. Write down the time before the day gets away from you. Preserve payment records before trying to reconstruct them from memory. Keep the platform report confirmation. Save the bank case number. Document who you spoke to and when.

For individuals, the first move when something suspicious happens should be simple: stop. Do not click more. Do not reply. Do not delete. Do not argue. Do not panic-send money. Preserve what happened. Write down the time. Verify through another channel. If passwords need to be changed, do it from a safe device. If money, phone access, banking, social media, email, or identity is involved, contact the bank, platform, carrier, or trusted support channel quickly.

The first goal is to preserve and contain.

For businesses, the same idea applies with more structure. Preserve evidence. Freeze high-risk actions if needed. Use a clean communication channel if email may be compromised. Notify the right internal person. Start the timeline. Avoid public or customer statements until the facts are clear. If money is involved, pause payment activity. If payroll or vendor banking is involved, freeze changes until verified. If customer data may be involved, preserve facts before guessing publicly.

Speed matters, but uncontrolled speed creates more damage.

This is where modern protection has to evolve. A good security system should not only warn people. It should help preserve evidence, build a timeline, explain what matters, and give the user a clean path from alert to response. Protection is not only detection. Protection is proof, response, recovery, and prevention.

That is the Aetis principle in this area. A protection system should help the user answer the questions that matter under pressure. What happened? What proof do we have? What could disappear? What needs to be preserved before action? Is money involved? Is identity involved? Is access involved? Is reputation involved? Is legal exposure involved? Is customer data involved? Should something be frozen until verified? Who needs to know? What is the next safest action?

That kind of guidance matters because panic-driven deletion is common. People want to clean up the mess, but cleanup before documentation can hurt recovery. The right system should help people preserve first, then respond. It should not drown them in technical language. It should help them understand what evidence matters, why it matters, and what to do next.

This is especially important for small businesses. A small business may not have a legal department, a security team, a public-relations team, and an insurance response team ready to move. The owner may be the person discovering the fake invoice, calling the bank, checking the email, calming the vendor, warning employees, and trying not to lose customers. In that environment, proof keeps the owner from operating only on fear.

Proof also helps with reputation. When something goes wrong, people often make assumptions. Customers may assume the business was careless. Vendors may assume the invoice was ignored. Employees may assume someone will be blamed. The public may assume the fake profile was real. Evidence gives the business a way to separate what happened from what people assume happened.

That does not mean every detail should be shared publicly. Sometimes legal, insurance, or security guidance is needed before communication. But internal proof gives leadership a better foundation. You cannot communicate clearly if you do not know the timeline. You cannot correct misinformation if you did not preserve the fake. You cannot prove responsible action if no one documented what was done.

Proof is not only for after the incident. It should be built into normal operations. A payment approval should not disappear into a casual text. A vendor banking change should not live only inside an email thread. A payroll change should have a record. An admin change should be logged. A public statement should have an approval path. A customer-data export should not be invisible. High-risk actions should leave enough evidence that the business can defend its decisions later.

That is not paperwork for the sake of paperwork. It is protection.

There will always be people who say, 'We are too small for that.' But small businesses often need proof the most because they have less room for confusion. One disputed payment can hurt cash flow. One fake page can damage trust. One employee mistake can become personal. One vendor dispute can turn into a legal or insurance problem. The smaller the business, the more important it is to preserve facts before the story gets messy.

The same is true for individuals. If your social account is taken over, proof helps you warn contacts. If your bank account is targeted, proof helps the bank understand the sequence. If a fake profile uses your photos, proof helps the platform see the impersonation. If someone claims you sent a message you did not send, proof helps show the account was compromised. If a family scam occurs, proof can help protect the next person who might be targeted.

Evidence gives you the ability to move from emotion to action.

That is the real message of this chapter. When something suspicious happens, do not rush to erase it. Do not delete the message before saving it. Do not close the page before capturing it. Do not block the fake profile before documenting it. Do not change everything before writing down what changed. Stop. Preserve. Write down the time. Save what matters. Then respond.

When something goes wrong, the person with proof has options. The person without proof has confusion.

In cybersecurity, evidence is not paperwork. Evidence is power.

Chapter 23

Recovery Is Part of Security

Recovery matters. But recovery is not the first move.

That is where too many security conversations get out of order. Yes, recovery is part of security. Yes, every person and every business needs to know how to recover when something goes wrong. But if we talk about recovery before we talk about closing doors, we make it sound like the plan is to get hit and clean up afterward.

That is not security. That is waiting for damage.

The first job is defense. Close the obvious doors. Reduce the number of ways someone can get in. Control the accounts. Remove the old access. Stop using five different systems when two would do the job. Protect the email. Protect the phone. Protect the payroll system. Protect the domain. Protect the bank. Protect the tools that hold customer data. Then, after you have reduced the open doors, you build recovery for what still gets through.

That is the order: close doors first, then plan recovery.

This chapter still belongs in the book because recovery is real. Something can still happen even when you are careful. A vendor can be compromised. A password can leak. A phone can be stolen. An employee can click. A platform can make a mistake. A fake invoice can slip into a busy day. Security is never a promise that nothing bad will ever happen. But that does not mean we surrender the front door and focus only on cleaning up the mess.

We have to play defense.

If your house has twenty open windows, a broken garage door, a spare key under the mat, and strangers walking through the backyard, you do not start by buying a better insurance policy and calling that safety. Insurance may matter. A recovery plan may matter. But the first sane move is to close the windows, lock the garage, move the spare key, and find out who has access to the property. Then you make sure you know what to do if something still goes wrong.

Digital security works the same way. The more doors you have into your personal life or business, the more likely someone will find one that is weak, forgotten, or unguarded. Every account is a door. Every app is a door. Every vendor portal is a door. Every old employee login is a door. Every shared password is a door. Every connected tool is a door. Every recovery email, phone number, cloud folder, payment processor, social media admin, and domain account is a door. Some doors are necessary. Some are useful. Some should have been closed a long time ago.

Recovery cannot be an excuse for leaving those doors open.

A person or business that says, "We have backups," but still has reused passwords, no multi-factor authentication, old devices, forgotten accounts, and uncontrolled access is not secure. A company that says, "We have cyber insurance," but lets one email change vendor banking details is not secure. A family that says, "We can reset the account," but has no idea who controls the recovery phone number is not secure. Recovery without defense is not a strategy. It is a reaction.

That is why this chapter should not be read as a soft landing after the hard truth of the earlier chapters. It should be read as a discipline. Recovery is part of security, but only after security has done its first job: reducing the attack surface.

Attack surface is just a technical way of saying, how many ways can someone reach you? How many accounts can they try? How many apps can they abuse? How many people can they impersonate? How many vendors can they hide behind? How many tools hold your data? How many old logins still work? How many passwords are reused? How many public details can be used to trick you?

How many places does money move? How many systems would you have to check if something went wrong?

If the answer is too many, recovery becomes harder before the attack even starts.

That is one of the reasons tool sprawl, personal oversharing, weak passwords, unmanaged vendors, and old accounts are so dangerous. They do not just create more chances for an attack. They make recovery messier when an attack happens. If you do not know what doors exist, you cannot know which one was used. If you do not know who has access, you cannot know who should be removed. If you do not know where files live, you cannot know what was exposed. If you do not know which account controls recovery, you cannot know whether the attacker still has a way back in.

So before we talk about recovery, we have to talk about control.

Control starts with knowing what you use. For an individual, that means knowing the accounts that matter most: email, phone, banking, cloud storage, social media, password manager, payment apps, tax accounts, medical portals, school accounts, and anything tied to your identity. For a business, it means knowing the systems that keep the company alive: owner email, finance email, payroll, banking, accounting, domain, website, social media pages, customer records, cloud files, payment processors, vendor portals, HR, insurance, contracts, and admin dashboards.

That does not mean every account has the same risk. It means you have to know which accounts are doors into the rest of your life or company. The email account that resets everything is a major door. The phone that receives codes is a major door. The payroll system is a major door. The domain registrar is a major door. The bank account is a major door. The social media page that speaks to your customers is a major door. Those doors need stronger locks before you ever talk about recovery.

Defense means using unique passwords. It means turning on stronger authentication. It means removing old users. It means reviewing app permissions.

It means protecting the phone carrier account. It means closing old accounts. It means limiting employee and vendor access. It means stopping payment changes from happening through one email. It means not letting one personal phone control the entire business. It means not letting one forgotten account become the doorway criminals use to walk in.

That is not complicated theory. That is basic defense.

A lot of people want to skip this part because it feels boring. They would rather talk about recovery tools, artificial intelligence, advanced monitoring, or the dramatic part of cybercrime. But boring security is often the security that works. A closed account cannot be logged into. A removed employee cannot use old access. A unique password cannot be reused from a breach somewhere else. A verified vendor change cannot be hijacked as easily. A tested backup is stronger than a hopeful one. A known recovery contact is better than searching during panic.

The more doors you close before the incident, the fewer doors you have to inspect after it.

That line is the bridge between defense and recovery. Recovery becomes stronger when defense has already reduced the mess. If a business has clear access, known vendors, documented payment rules, protected email, controlled cloud storage, and fewer unmanaged tools, then recovery has a starting point. The owner can ask, what changed? Who had access? What account was affected? What system matters first? What do we still control?

If the business is a pile of disconnected tools, recovery begins with confusion. Nobody knows which account is official. Nobody knows who owns the vendor portal. Nobody knows whether the old contractor still has access. Nobody knows whether cloud sync is a backup. Nobody knows whether the domain is controlled by the business or by someone's personal email. Nobody knows which payment link is real. In that kind of environment, recovery is slower because the business has to map the doors while the fire is already burning.

That is why prevention and recovery cannot be separated. Defense reduces the number of doors. Recovery tells you what to do if someone still gets through one. You need both, but they are not equal in sequence. You do not build recovery as a replacement for defense. You build recovery on top of defense.

For a person, that might mean protecting the email and phone first. If those two are weak, everything else is fragile. Then protect banking, social media, cloud storage, and the accounts that control identity. Remove old apps. Review recovery settings. Stop sharing codes. Clean up old accounts. Limit what strangers can learn from public posts. After that, build a recovery plan: know how to contact the bank, know how to reach the phone carrier, know where recovery codes are stored, know how to warn contacts, and know what to preserve if something suspicious happens.

For a business, the same order applies. First, close doors. Know the tools. Know who has access. Remove former employees. Reduce duplicate systems. Protect owner, finance, payroll, domain, cloud, bank, website, and social media access. Verify vendor banking changes. Require stronger authentication. Stop using shared passwords for critical systems. Make sure payments, payroll, admin changes, and vendor changes do not happen invisibly. Then build recovery around the remaining critical doors.

That is what mature security looks like. Not fear. Not chaos. Not buying every tool. Discipline.

Recovery is still part of the plan because no defense is perfect. But the purpose of recovery is not to excuse weak defense. The purpose of recovery is to restore control when a controlled environment is disrupted. That is a very different message from, "Something will happen anyway, so just be ready to recover." The better message is, "Close as many doors as you can, strengthen the doors you must keep, and know how to recover if one still fails."

This matters because criminals look for the easiest path. They do not always need to break the strongest system. They look for the old account, the reused password, the unprotected phone number, the vendor process that runs by email alone, the cloud folder nobody owns, the former employee still logged in, the business page controlled by one personal account, or the recovery email that no one checks anymore. These are not exotic attacks. These are open doors.

A person can have a recovery plan and still be too exposed. A business can have backups and still be too exposed. A company can have insurance and still be too exposed. Recovery is strongest when it starts from a place of reduced exposure, not from a wide-open environment.

Think about the business owner whose email is compromised. In the weaker version of the story, the owner changes the password and thinks everything is fixed. But the attacker left behind forwarding rules and connected apps. The owner did not close the doors. They only changed one lock. Weeks later, the attacker watches a vendor conversation and sends fake payment instructions. The business loses money because the recovery was incomplete.

Now imagine the stronger version. Before anything ever happened, the business had already reduced the doors. Vendor banking changes required known-channel verification. Finance accounts had strong authentication. Email forwarding rules were reviewed regularly. Payment changes required approval outside the email thread. The vendor master record was documented. Former users had been removed. When the email compromise was discovered, recovery still mattered, but the attacker had fewer ways to turn that compromise into a larger disaster.

That is the point. Defense does not guarantee nothing will happen. Defense limits what can happen next.

Recovery also has to be clean. Getting back in is not recovery if the attacker still has a path back. Restoring a file is not recovery if the same ransomware can reach the backup. Unlocking a social media account is not recovery if fake posts and fake profiles are still damaging trust. Calling the bank is not recovery if the payment process that allowed fraud stays the same. Recovery is not just getting the thing back. Recovery is restoring control and closing the path that failed.

That is why every incident should ask two questions. First, what door did they use? Second, how do we close or strengthen that door before we move on?

If a password was reused, the answer is not only to change that password. It is to stop the reuse. If a vendor email was compromised, the answer is not only to warn the vendor. It is to verify payment changes through a known channel from now on. If a former employee still had access, the answer is not only to remove that employee. It is to fix offboarding. If a cloud folder was exposed, the answer is not only to change the link. It is to review folder ownership and sharing rules. If a phone number was taken over, the answer is not only to get the number back. It is to protect the carrier account and move critical accounts away from weak recovery methods where possible.

Recovery that does not improve defense is just cleanup.

This is why I do not want readers to leave this chapter thinking recovery is a comfort blanket. It is not. Recovery is a command function. It is what you use when something has broken, but it only works well if the business or person has already done the defensive work. You cannot recover cleanly from a situation you do not understand. You cannot restore control if you do not know who had control. You cannot prove what changed if nothing left a trail. You cannot close the door if you do not know where the door is.

Evidence still matters here. Logs still matter. Timelines still matter. But they should serve defense and recovery together. A log can show what changed. A timeline can show when the attack began. A screenshot can prove what was sent. A payment record can show where money went. Those facts help recovery, but they also help the person or business strengthen the next layer of defense.

That is the right relationship between proof, defense, and recovery. Proof shows what happened. Defense closes what should not stay open. Recovery restores what was damaged. Prevention reduces the next opportunity. They are not separate pieces. They are one cycle.

A modern protection system should follow that cycle. It should not only alert someone that something is wrong. It should help them understand what door is involved, what needs to be preserved, what must be frozen, what account controls recovery, what action is safe, and what door has to be closed after the immediate danger is handled. The goal should be less exposure, better proof, cleaner recovery, and stronger prevention next time.

That is the Aetis principle in this area: protection is not only detection, and recovery is not only cleanup. Protection is reducing doors, preserving proof, restoring control, and preventing the same path from staying open.

For individuals, that means a recovery plan should begin before the crisis. Know your critical accounts. Protect the recovery email and phone. Store recovery codes safely. Know official bank and carrier contacts. Clean up old accounts. Review devices. Use stronger authentication. Back up important files in a way you can actually restore. Talk to family about emergency scams. Those steps are defense first, recovery second, and both are necessary.

For businesses, the same truth is larger. Know your critical systems. Know who owns them. Know who has access. Know which systems can move money, change payroll, speak publicly, hold customer data, or control recovery. Close unused tools. Remove old access. Verify vendors. Protect finance and payroll. Test backups. Create a clean communication path. Know who makes decisions during an incident. Document what matters. Then, if something still happens, recovery begins from a position of control instead of chaos.

A business recovery plan is not just about computers. It is about keeping the business alive while the door that failed is being closed. That means money movement may need to pause. Vendor changes may need to freeze. Payroll may need special verification. Customer communication may need to be careful and factual. Email may not be a trusted channel if email is compromised. Public statements may need to wait until the timeline is clear. Recovery is not panic. Recovery is controlled action.

But again, controlled action is only possible when the doors are known.

That is why this chapter belongs after the chapters on baselines, fewer tools, and evidence. The order matters. First, know the baseline. Then reduce the doors. Then preserve proof. Then recover. If we reverse that order, we teach people to clean up messes instead of preventing as many messes as possible.

Recovery is not what happens because you stopped playing defense. Recovery is what happens because even good defense needs a plan for the moment something gets through.

That is the difference. A weak security mindset says, "Something bad will probably happen, so we will recover later." A stronger security mindset says, "We will close the doors we can, guard the doors we need, monitor the doors that matter, preserve proof if something changes, and recover quickly if one door still fails."

That is not pessimism. That is maturity.

The reader should leave this chapter with a stronger idea than simple recovery. The goal is not to be wide open and recover well. The goal is to be hard to enter, hard to move through, hard to impersonate, hard to confuse, and hard to keep compromised. If something does happen, then recovery restores control and strengthens the defense that should have been there in the first place.

Security is not only prevention, but prevention comes first. Recovery is not a replacement for defense. It is the discipline that proves the defense can bend without breaking.

Close the doors. Control the keys. Preserve the proof. Then recover what still gets hit.

Recovery is not what happens after security fails. Recovery is part of security because defense and recovery have to work together.

Chapter 24

The Cybersecurity Program Every Business Needs

A cybersecurity program is not a pile of tools.

That is the first thing every business owner needs to understand. A password manager can be useful. Antivirus can be useful. Backups can be useful. Cyber insurance can be useful. Email filtering, endpoint protection, cloud security, device management, fraud alerts, and monitoring tools can all be useful. But none of those things, by themselves, make a business secure.

Tools are pieces. A program is the way those pieces are used.

A business does not become secure because it owns security software. It becomes secure when cybersecurity becomes part of how the business makes decisions, grants access, moves money, verifies requests, preserves proof, and recovers when something goes wrong. The program is not the app. The program is the operating discipline behind the app.

That difference matters because many businesses buy tools and then assume the problem is handled. They install something, subscribe to something, get a login, receive a few alerts, and feel like they have checked the cybersecurity box. But when a fake vendor invoice arrives, nobody knows who should verify it. When an employee leaves, nobody removes every login. When the owner loses access to email, nobody knows which account controls recovery. When a social media page is cloned, nobody knows who owns the official channel. When a payment is redirected, nobody knows whether the payment change was approved.

That is not a cybersecurity program. That is a collection of tools sitting on top of a weak process.

Every business needs a cybersecurity program, but not every business needs an enterprise-level department. A solo founder does not need the same structure as a global company. A local shop does not need the same program as a bank. A creator, contractor, nonprofit, medical office, salon, construction company, restaurant, consulting firm, or small online business may not need a full security staff. But every one of them still needs rules.

Who has access? Who can move money? Who verifies vendor changes? Who owns the domain? Who controls social media? What gets logged? What happens if email is compromised? What happens if payroll is attacked? What happens if the business is locked out of a critical account? What happens if a customer receives a fake message using the business name?

That is the program.

Cybersecurity is no longer just protecting computers. It is protecting the way the business runs.

That sentence is the center of this final full chapter. Cybersecurity affects finance, payroll, HR, vendor management, customer communication, legal exposure, insurance, reputation, operations, and recovery. If a business owner treats cybersecurity as only an IT problem, they will miss the places where real damage happens. A fake invoice may not look like a computer problem. A payroll change may not look like a network attack. A cloned business page may not look like malware. A compromised vendor email may not look like hacking. But each one can hurt the business in a very real way.

The cybersecurity program every business needs should protect the things that keep the business alive. It should protect money, payroll, email, customer records, employee records, vendor relationships, the domain name, the website, social media, cloud files, contracts, bank accounts, payment processors, business reputation, recovery paths, and decision-making. It should protect systems, but it should also protect trust.

Because if trust breaks, the business suffers even if the computers still turn on.

A company can lose trust without losing a single laptop. A customer can receive a fake invoice and lose confidence. A vendor can be impersonated and create a payment dispute. An employee can be blamed because no one preserved proof. A social page can be taken over and confuse the public. A fake support account can scam customers using the business name. A single wrong message can make people question whether the business is safe to work with.

That is why cybersecurity has to move from the side of the business to the center of operations.

A real program begins by knowing the doors. A business cannot protect systems it does not know it uses. It cannot remove access it does not know exists. It cannot recover an account if nobody knows what email or phone controls recovery. It cannot secure customer data if nobody knows where the data lives. It cannot stop a fake payment if nobody knows what a real payment process looks like.

The first responsibility of a cybersecurity program is visibility.

What accounts exist? What tools are used? What devices connect? What vendors have access? What employees have logins? What cloud folders hold customer data? What email controls recovery? What dashboard can move money? What social media account speaks for the business? What system controls payroll? What platform holds contracts? What app stores customer conversations? What old tool still has active users even though nobody uses it anymore?

You cannot lock a door you forgot existed.

Once the business knows its doors, the next responsibility is controlling access. Access is not about whether people are trusted. Access is about what their role actually needs. That distinction is important because business owners often confuse trust with access. They trust the employee, so they give broad access.

They trust the contractor, so they leave a folder open. They trust the assistant, so they share passwords. They trust the vendor, so they do not review permissions. Then months later, nobody knows who can still touch what.

A good program does not give unlimited access because someone is trusted. It gives the right access, to the right person, for the right reason, for the right amount of time.

Trust people. Control access.

That applies to employees, vendors, contractors, assistants, bookkeepers, finance users, payroll users, social media admins, domain admins, and former employees. The former employee part matters because access does not disappear just because the relationship ends. If the login still works, the door is still open. Offboarding is not paperwork. It is security. When someone leaves, access should end before the relationship fully ends, not days or weeks later.

The same discipline applies to vendors. A vendor relationship is not proof that every vendor request is real. Vendors can be impersonated. Vendors can be compromised. Vendors can make mistakes. A vendor may be legitimate, but the email using that vendor's name may not be. A program should know who the real vendors are, who the real contacts are, what systems vendors can access, what data they handle, and how payment changes are verified.

A business does not need to distrust vendors. It needs vendor controls.

Verification is another major part of the program. Anything that can move money, expose data, change access, damage reputation, or create legal risk should be verified before action. That includes money movement, payroll changes, vendor banking changes, admin access, legal threats, customer data requests, public statements, account recovery, domain changes, payment processor changes, and social media ownership.

Verification is not distrust. Verification is how the business protects trust.

A business can survive inconvenience better than it can survive uncontrolled money movement. That may sound blunt, but it is true. A delayed payment can be explained. A stolen payment can threaten cash flow, vendor relationships, insurance claims, legal position, and trust. Fake invoices, vendor banking changes, payroll fraud, refund fraud, fake owner requests, fake executive approvals, and compromised vendor emails all target the same thing: money leaving before anyone slows down.

A cybersecurity program should make money movement harder to fake.

No one email should move money. No one urgent message should change payroll. No vendor banking change should happen without known-channel verification. No emergency request should bypass approval because someone sounded important. Money needs rules. Not because employees cannot be trusted, but because criminals know how to borrow trust and turn it into pressure.

The program also has to protect business identity. Business identity is more than a logo. It includes the domain, website, official email, social media pages, public statements, brand reputation, customer trust, and the channels people use to know what is real. If criminals take over or clone those channels, they can scam customers, redirect payments, damage the brand, spread fake statements, or impersonate the company.

A business cybersecurity program should protect the company's name, voice, and official channels.

If customers cannot tell what is real, trust becomes vulnerable. That is why the domain registrar matters. That is why social media ownership matters. That is why official contact channels matter. That is why business email should not be controlled by one personal account that only one person understands. That is why public-facing accounts need stronger protection. The business has to know who can speak for it, where official messages come from, and how fake channels are reported when they appear.

Employees are part of the security program, but they are not the enemy. This book has said that in different ways throughout the chapters because it matters. Employees should not be expected to carry the whole security burden alone. A program should give them clear rules, safe tools, permission to slow down, and a safe way to report.

An employee should know what should be verified. They should know who to ask. They should know what not to share. They should know that codes are keys. They should know how to report a suspicious message. They should know what to do after a mistake. They should know that a payment request from the owner still follows the payment rule. They should know that asking a question is not being difficult. It is protecting the business.

A good program protects employees from being the last line of defense by themselves.

This is where leadership matters. A cybersecurity program fails if leadership treats it as someone else's problem. Owners and executives must follow the same rules, especially around payment approval, access, vendor changes, payroll, legal threats, and verification. Leadership cannot say, "Everyone else must verify, but I can bypass the process." That weakens the whole program.

Security culture starts at the top.

If the owner ignores the rules, employees will learn that rules are flexible. If executives approve payments through casual messages, criminals will imitate that behavior. If leadership shames people for slowing down, employees will move faster than they should. If leaders punish honest reporting, people will hide mistakes. The program is not only what is written down. It is what leadership actually allows.

A business that punishes fast reporting trains people to hide. A business that protects fast reporting gets the truth sooner.

No-shame reporting does not mean no accountability. It means the first priority is containment, evidence, and truth. If someone clicks something, shares something, or notices something strange, the business needs to know quickly. If people hide mistakes, attackers get more time. Evidence disappears. Recovery gets harder. A culture that protects fast reporting protects the company.

Evidence and logs belong inside the program for the same reason. High-risk actions should leave a trail. Not to spy on people. To know what happened when money, access, trust, or reputation is at risk. Payments should leave a trail. Payroll changes should leave a trail. Vendor changes should leave a trail. Admin changes should leave a trail. Access requests should leave a trail. Public statements should leave a trail.

When something goes wrong, logs and evidence turn confusion into a timeline.

That timeline matters to banks, insurers, vendors, platforms, lawyers, customers, employees, and leadership. It can show whether a process was followed. It can show when access changed. It can show whether a vendor request was abnormal. It can show who approved a payment. It can show when a fake profile appeared. It can show whether the business acted responsibly. Evidence is not paperwork for the sake of paperwork. Evidence is what gives the business options when the story gets messy.

Recovery also belongs in the program, but in the right order. Close doors first. Play defense. Then build recovery for what still gets through.

Recovery is not an excuse to leave doors open. Recovery is the discipline that helps the business restore control when good defense still gets tested. A strong program does not say, "We have backups, so we do not need prevention." It says, "We reduce risk first. We defend what matters. We preserve proof. And if something still happens, we recover with discipline."

That corrected order matters. If a business has too many doors, unclear access, forgotten tools, weak passwords, uncontrolled vendor requests, and no payment rules, recovery will be chaotic. The business will spend the crisis trying to understand its own systems. But if the business has already closed unnecessary doors, controlled access, documented ownership, verified high-risk actions, and preserved evidence, recovery starts from a stronger position.

A small business cybersecurity program should be simple enough to use, but serious enough to protect the company. It should cover accounts, access, money, employees, vendors, devices, files, evidence, reporting, and recovery. It does not need to be complicated. It needs to be real.

The owner should know what systems exist. The owner should know who has access. The owner should know how money is approved. The owner should know how vendors are verified. The owner should know how employees report issues. The owner should know how evidence is saved. The owner should know how recovery begins.

That is enough to start.

As the business grows, the program has to mature. Informal trust may work when two people sit in the same room, but it does not scale well when the company adds employees, vendors, contractors, remote tools, customer records, payroll complexity, social media channels, insurance requirements, and compliance expectations. A growing business needs more structure. It needs formal access reviews, documented approval rules, vendor risk review, audit logs, a training schedule, an incident plan, backup testing, cyber insurance review, leadership reporting, role-based permissions, and clearer separation of duties.

As the business grows, the system has to grow with it.

At the enterprise level, cybersecurity becomes operational resilience. The organization needs formal governance, incident command, executive visibility, vendor risk management, legal and insurance coordination, audit trails, continuity planning, role-based accountability, business-wide recovery, and leadership-level reporting. At that level, cybersecurity is not just protection. It is how the organization keeps functioning under pressure.

The level of formality changes, but the foundation does not. Know the doors. Control the keys. Verify what matters. Preserve proof. Recover with discipline. Keep improving.

That is also the direction modern cybersecurity has to move. The future is not more noise. It is not more disconnected dashboards. It is not more alerts nobody understands. The future is one clearer way for a business to see what matters and act before confusion becomes damage. The business needs a control layer that helps it see its doors, control its keys, verify high-risk actions, preserve proof, and recover without chaos.

That is the Aetis philosophy: more control, less chaos, fewer unmanaged doors, better proof, and cleaner recovery.

This is not a product pitch. It is the natural evolution of the problem. Businesses are already overwhelmed by tools. They do not need ten more places to look. They need a way to know what is open, what matters, what changed, who has access, what should be verified, what proof exists, and what has to happen next.

Business owners should stop buying tools without process. Stop letting one email move money. Stop leaving former users active. Stop treating vendor requests as automatically real. Stop using personal accounts for business control. Stop ignoring social media ownership. Stop letting one phone control everything. Stop waiting until something goes wrong. Stop assuming the business is too small to be targeted. Stop thinking a tool replaces discipline. Stop allowing access nobody owns. Stop letting recovery depend on memory.

Security gaps are often ordinary business habits left unmanaged.

Business owners should start documenting critical accounts. Start removing old access. Start verifying payment changes. Start protecting recovery paths. Start training employees without shame. Start testing backups. Start preserving evidence. Start reviewing vendors. Start limiting admin access. Start using stronger authentication. Start documenting who owns what. Start treating cybersecurity as operating discipline.

The goal is not perfection. The goal is control.

Consider the business owner who thinks they have cybersecurity because they bought several tools. They have payroll software, accounting software, cloud storage, a customer system, social media tools, email security, a payment processor, a scheduling app, and a project management system. On paper, it looks like a modern business. There are tools everywhere.

Then a fake vendor invoice appears.

Nobody knows which system is official. Nobody knows who approved the vendor. Nobody knows whether the payment change was verified. Nobody knows who still has access. Nobody knows which email controls recovery. Nobody knows whether the vendor contact is real. Nobody knows where the evidence is. Nobody knows whether the former bookkeeper still has access.

The business did not have a cybersecurity program. It had tools.

Now compare that to a business with a program. It may still use tools, but the tools are governed. The business has fewer unmanaged doors. Critical accounts have owners. Vendor contacts are known. Payment changes are verified. Access is reviewed. Former users are removed. Evidence leaves a trail. Recovery has a starting point. Employees can report without shame. Leadership follows the same rules as everyone else.

That business may still face risk. Every connected business does. But it is not operating blind.

That is what the reader should take from this final full chapter. A business does not become secure because it owns security tools. It becomes secure when cybersecurity becomes part of how the business operates every day. Security is not separate from the business. It is how the business protects trust, money, people, reputation, and continuity.

This should not leave you afraid. It should leave you grounded. The path is clear enough to begin. Know your doors. Control your keys. Verify what matters. Preserve proof. Recover with discipline. Keep improving.

Cybersecurity is not impossible. It is not reserved for giant companies. It is not something only technical people are allowed to understand. It is a discipline the business builds one decision at a time.

Cybersecurity is not a product you buy once. It is a discipline you build into the way your business survives, earns trust, and keeps moving.

Conclusion

You Are Not Powerless

The age of exposure is real.

Your email, phone, bank, business, family, social media, vendors, files, passwords, public records, and reputation are all connected now. That connection creates convenience, but it also creates doors. Some doors are necessary. Some doors are useful. Some doors should have been closed a long time ago.

But here is the part I want you to remember:

You are not powerless.

Cybersecurity can feel overwhelming because the threat feels bigger than one person, one family, or one business. The scams are cleaner. The messages look real. The voices can sound familiar. The websites can look professional. The invoices can look normal. The criminals move fast, and the systems we depend on are not always built to protect the average person in a way they can understand.

But powerless is not the same as unprepared.

You may not be able to control every breach, every platform, every vendor, every scammer, or every new technology. But you can control more than you think. You can close doors. You can protect your email. You can protect your phone. You can stop reusing important passwords. You can turn on stronger authentication. You can verify before money moves. You can slow down when pressure appears. You can preserve proof before deleting evidence. You can teach employees and family members without shame. You can remove access that no longer belongs. You can reduce tools that create confusion. You can build recovery after you have played defense.

That is power.

Not dramatic power. Practical power.

The power to stop being easy to process. The power to know what matters. The power to say, "We verify that here." The power to tell an employee, "Thank you for reporting quickly." The power to tell your family, "If an emergency message comes in, we check before we act." The power to look at your business and ask, "Who has the keys, and which doors can we close?"

This book was never about making you afraid of technology. It was about helping you see the world clearly. Cybersecurity is no longer just about computers. It is about trust. It is about money. It is about people. It is about reputation. It is about keeping your life and business from being used against you.

The invisible war becomes less invisible when you know what to look for.

A scam does not need to look fake to be fake. A voice does not have to be real to sound real. A vendor message does not have to be legitimate because the name is familiar. A professional-looking website does not prove safety. A rushed request does not deserve blind trust. A tool does not create security by itself. Recovery does not replace defense.

The answer is discipline.

Know your doors. Control your keys. Verify what matters. Preserve proof. Close what should not be open. Recover with discipline when something still gets through. Then improve.

You do not have to become perfect. You do not have to become paranoid. You do not have to become a cybersecurity expert overnight.

But you do have to become aware.

Because in the age of exposure, the safest people are not the ones who pretend nothing can happen. They are the ones who understand that something can happen, prepare before it does, and refuse to remain wide open.

You are not powerless.

You are exposed only until you start closing doors.

Afterword

Security Is Trust

By the time you reach the end of this book, one truth should be clear:

Cybersecurity is not only about technology.

It is about trust.

It is about whether a person can trust the message in front of them. Whether a business can trust the invoice it receives. Whether an employee can trust the request that appears to come from the owner. Whether a parent can trust the voice on the phone. Whether a customer can trust the company page they are messaging. Whether a founder can trust the opportunity in front of them. Whether a community can trust the systems it depends on.

That is what cybercrime attacks.

Not just passwords.

Not just computers.

Not just bank accounts.

Not just data.

Cybercrime attacks trust.

It borrows the name of a bank.

It borrows the voice of a loved one.

It borrows the logo of a company.

It borrows the tone of a boss.

It borrows the reputation of a vendor.

It borrows the urgency of an emergency.

It borrows the hope of an opportunity.

Then it uses that borrowed trust to make people act before they verify.

That is why the old way of thinking about cybersecurity is no longer enough.

For years, people were taught to think of cybersecurity as something technical, distant, and optional. Something for IT departments. Something for banks. Something for large corporations. Something for people with servers, not families. Something for enterprises, not small businesses. Something for experts, not ordinary people trying to live, work, build, parent, lead, serve, and survive in a connected world.

But the world changed.

Your email is now a front door.

Your phone is now a master key.

Your social media is now part of your identity.

Your business tools are now operational doors.

Your vendor relationships are now attack paths.

Your public information is now research material.

Your reputation can be cloned.

Your voice can be copied.

Your company can be impersonated.

Your trust can be weaponized.

And when that is the world we live in, security cannot remain a side task.

Security has to become part of how we live.

Part of how we run businesses.

Part of how we protect families.

Part of how we train employees.

Part of how we verify money movement.

Part of how we choose tools.

Part of how we preserve proof.

Part of how we recover.

Part of how we keep going.

That is the reason Aetis exists.

Aetis was not built from the belief that people are careless. It was built from the belief that people are human.

People get tired.

People get rushed.

People want to help.

People trust familiar names.

People hope an opportunity is real.

People fear losing access, money, reputation, or time.

People make decisions under pressure.

And criminals know that.

So the answer cannot be shame.

The answer cannot be more noise.

The answer cannot be another disconnected dashboard people ignore.

The answer cannot be expecting every person to become a cybersecurity expert overnight.

The answer has to be a system that understands the real world.

A system that knows security is not only about stopping malware. It is about protecting identity, money, access, evidence, reputation, communication, vendors, employees, families, and recovery.

Aetis is built around that idea.

At the personal level, protection should help people understand their baseline: email, phone, passwords, MFA, banking, social media, cloud files, recovery codes, family safety, and privacy exposure. A person should not have to guess whether they are wide open. They should be able to see what matters and what needs attention.

At the small-business level, protection should help owners see the business clearly: which tools they use, who has access, which vendors are real, who can move money, who controls payroll, who owns the domain, which accounts still have old users, which files are exposed, and what happens when something goes wrong.

At the high-profile and public-facing level, protection has to include reputation, identity, impersonation, fake profiles, deepfakes, private communication, official channels, and the reality that a person's name, face, voice, audience, and trust can all be targeted.

At the enterprise level, protection has to become operational discipline: governance, continuity, incident command, audit trails, executive visibility, vendor risk, recovery coordination, legal readiness, and the ability to keep the organization moving under pressure.

That is the larger vision.

Not just alerts.

Not just antivirus.

Not just password reminders.

Not just another app.

Aetis is built as a control layer for trust.

A way to see the doors.

Control the keys.

Verify what matters.

Preserve proof.

Recover with discipline.

And keep improving.

Because security without trust becomes fear.

But trust without verification becomes risk.

The future belongs somewhere in the middle.

We should still trust people. Families need trust. Businesses need trust. Employees need trust. Customers need trust. Vendors need trust. Communities need trust. No one can live or lead in a world where everything is treated as hostile all the time.

But trust has to grow up.

Trust now needs process.

Trust needs proof.

Trust needs clean channels.

Trust needs access boundaries.

Trust needs logs.

Trust needs recovery plans.

Trust needs the courage to slow down when pressure goes up.

That does not make trust weaker.

It makes trust survivable.

A business that verifies vendor changes is not insulting its vendors. It is protecting the relationship.

A family that uses an emergency phrase is not distrusting each other. It is protecting each other from panic.

An employee who questions an urgent payment request is not being difficult. They are protecting the business.

A founder who verifies an investor outside the provided documents is not being paranoid. They are protecting the future they are building.

A public figure who monitors impersonation is not being dramatic. They are protecting the trust people place in their name.

This is the shift.

Cybersecurity is no longer only about defense against strangers.

It is about protecting the systems of trust that make life and business possible.

That is why proof matters.

That is why recovery matters.

That is why fewer unmanaged tools matter.

That is why access control matters.

That is why no-shame reporting matters.

That is why verification matters.

That is why privacy matters.

That is why every business, no matter its size, needs a cybersecurity program.

Not because every business needs to become a fortress overnight.

But because every business has something worth protecting.

A customer list.

A bank account.

A reputation.

A payroll system.

A domain name.

A vendor relationship.

A social media page.

A set of invoices.

A founder's name.

A community's trust.

A future.

Security is not about fear.

Fear freezes people.

Security should create calm.

The kind of calm that comes from knowing who has access. Knowing what to verify. Knowing where proof is stored. Knowing what to freeze. Knowing who to call. Knowing how to recover. Knowing that one mistake does not have to become a disaster.

That is what good security should do.

It should make people safer without making them feel powerless.

It should help employees report without shame.

It should help owners lead without guessing.

It should help families prepare without panic.

It should help public-facing people protect their identity without disappearing.

It should help businesses recover without chaos.

Because the goal is not to live scared.

The goal is to live awake.

To understand that the digital world is not separate from real life anymore. It is where money moves, trust forms, identities live, businesses operate, families communicate, reputations grow, and opportunities appear.

So protecting the digital world is no longer optional.

It is part of protecting life.

That is why this book was written.

Not to make you afraid of every message, every tool, every person, or every opportunity.

But to help you see the pattern.

To help you understand the doors.

To help you slow down when pressure rises.

To help you stop treating professional-looking scams as proof.

To help you protect the people connected to you.

To help you build a baseline.

To help you create a program.

To help you recover if something goes wrong.

To help you understand that cybersecurity is not about perfection.

It is about discipline.

The discipline to use unique passwords.
The discipline to verify payment changes.
The discipline to protect your phone.
The discipline to remove old access.
The discipline to preserve evidence.
The discipline to test backups.
The discipline to report quickly.
The discipline to build systems that protect people on their worst day, not only their best one.

That discipline is not glamorous.

But it is powerful.

It is what keeps a mistake from becoming a collapse.

It is what keeps confusion from becoming opportunity for criminals.

It is what keeps trust from becoming an open door.

And that is the final message:

Security is trust.

Not blind trust.

Not fearful trust.

Not trust based on appearance, urgency, authority, or hope.

Verified trust.

Trust with boundaries.

Trust with proof.

Trust with recovery.

Trust with accountability.

Trust that can survive pressure.

That is what we need now.

That is what individuals need.

That is what families need.

That is what small businesses need.

That is what public-facing people need.

That is what enterprises need.

That is what the future needs.

Because in the digital age, the question is not whether trust matters.

Trust matters more than ever.

The question is whether we will protect it.

And that is what security is for.

www.ingramcontent.com/pod-product-compliance
Lightning Source LLC
Chambersburg PA
CBHW020840150726
48196CB00002B/152
9798889900009